W9-BUB-876

# Basic
# BASKET MAKING

# Basic
# BASKET MAKING

## All the Skills and Tools You Need to Get Started

*Linda Franz, editor*

*Debra Hammond,*
*basket weaver*
*and consultant*

*photographs by*
*Alan Wycheck*

STACKPOLE
BOOKS

*Thanks to Debra Hammond for sharing her wonderful designs and basket expertise, and for allowing us to use her basket shop.*

*Thanks to Alan Wycheck for his photos and his advice.*

*And thanks to all the folks at Stackpole who helped put this book together— Mark Allison, Janelle Steen, Wendy Reynolds, and Caroline Stover.*

Copyright © 2008 by Stackpole Books

Published by
STACKPOLE BOOKS
5067 Ritter Road
Mechanicsburg, PA 17055
www.stackpolebooks.com

Printed in China

10  9  8  7  6  5  4  3  2  1

First edition

**Library of Congress Cataloging-in-Publication Data**

Basic basket making: all the skills and tools you need to get started / Linda Franz, editor ; Debra Hammond, basket weaver and consultant ; photographs by Alan Wycheck. — 1st ed.
        p. cm.
    ISBN-13: 978-0-8117-3488-2
    ISBN-10: 0-8117-3488-9
  1. Basket making. I. Franz, Linda. II. Hammond, Debra.

TT879.B3B363 2008
746.41'2—dc22
                                                        2007048096

# Contents

# Introduction

In this book we'll show and explain how to weave baskets using flat reed. Getting started in making these baskets requires few tools and equipment. In fact, most of the supplies, or their substitutes, can probably be found in your home.

Each of the four baskets illustrated teach different skills. You'll learn how to weave, how to twine, and how to make a basket with a handle. You'll learn how to make a round woven base, an open weave base, and a filled base; and you'll learn two techniques for finishing the top of a basket. Once the techniques are mastered, you can mix and match them to create your own unique baskets.

Reed in many colors and sizes can be purchased online, through mail order or from basket shops and some craft shops. Learn how to dye your own reed (see chapter 5) and you can create baskets in colors that match your home's decor.

Because many of the same skills are used in each of the baskets, begin by reading the instructions for starting and finishing. It is helpful to read the instructions for making the first basket before starting any of the other baskets.

Let's begin.

# Part I

---

# Tools and Materials

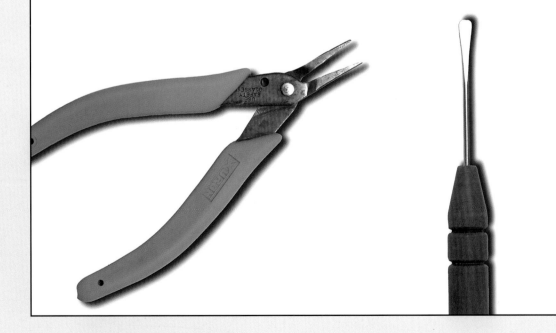

# TOOLS AND MATERIALS

While many specialized tools have been designed for the basket weaver, just a few are needed to complete the projects we'll make in this book. And many can be substituted with items you probably already have.

### CRIMPING TOOL

The crimping tool is used to bend round reed when a 90-degree angle is needed. By bending it with the crimping tool, the reed is less likely to break. You could substitute long-nose or needle-nose pliers for the crimping tool, but a crimping tool will provide a neater result.

### CRAFT SCISSORS

A good pair of craft scissors is needed to make clean cuts through reed. You'll use your scissors often as you cut spokes to length, clip weavers to fit behind a spoke, and trim ends to blend in with the basket.

### PACKING TOOL

The packing tool is used to "pack" woven reeds tightly together. It is also used to separate reeds so that another reed can be woven between them. To get started, you could substitute a screwdriver for the packing tool.

### TOWEL

An old towel is needed to dry dyed reed. Dyed reed can sometimes bleed its color onto other portions of the basket if it is not dried after soaking and before using.

2

## CLOTHESPINS

Clothespins are used to hold weaving in place, especially for the first row or two, to attach a rim before it is woven, and to hold reed together while it soaks. You'll need several of the type with a spring. These clothespins are plastic, but wooden clothespins also are suitable.

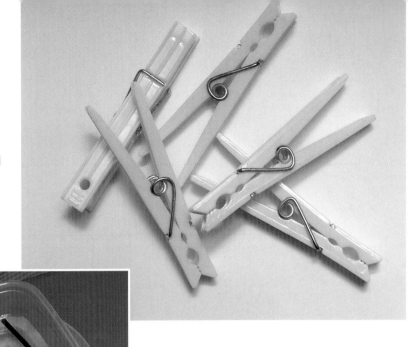

## PLASTIC CONTAINER

A plastic container is used to soak reed before weaving. Reed must be soaked to make it pliable and to prevent it from breaking while it is being woven. A plastic container is handy because it is sturdy, lightweight, and can be placed on your worktable, but another type of container could be used.

## YARDSTICK

You'll need a yardstick to measure lengths of reed. This folding yardstick is easy to store, and it can be used to measure short lengths as well as longer lengths.

HAMMOND BASKETS & WEAVING SUPPLIES
1709 Turkey Hill Rd., East Earl, PA 17519
Basket Weaving Classes
717-445-4653

## PENCIL

Got a pencil? You'll need it to mark your reed. This helps in assuring the baskets you make are symmetrical.

## Types of Reed

The reed used to weave baskets comes from the rattan plant. While hundreds of species of rattan exist, just a few species are used to produce the reed for baskets. Classified as a palm, the rattan plant vines through the tropical rain forest canopy.

The core of the rattan vine is used to produce round reed, flat reed, and flat oval reed. Most of the reed that is produced commercially comes from the rain forests of Indonesia and Southeast Asia.

The rattan core is processed and cut into the different types of reed and into varying widths. The finished reed is coiled and tied into 1-pound hanks. Each hank contains a single type and width of reed, such as ½" flat reed. The lengths of reed in each hank usually measure about 8 to 10 feet but can be longer or shorter.

Basket reed usually is sold in 1-pound hanks. Dyed reed also can be purchased in ¼-pound coils. Many basket craft shops and online suppliers sell basket kits that contain the amounts of reed needed to complete a specific basket.

Seagrass is often used as an accent in basket rims. It is a natural product made from grasses that grow on banks near the sea. Seagrass is twisted and coiled into 1-pound hanks.

All of the baskets in this book can be made using these weaving supplies:

⅝" flat reed
½" flat reed, natural and dyed
⅜" flat reed, natural and dyed
¼" flat reed, natural and dyed
¼" flat oval reed
#2 round reed
#3 round reed, dyed
#3 seagrass
6" D handles

## Preparing Reeds

Weaving supplies can be purchased online, through mail order, at basket shops, or in some craft stores. Check the yellow pages for basket shops and craft stores near you. You'll also find plenty of choices through an online search for "basket weaving supplies."

When you're ready to begin, work at a table with enough room to comfortably measure and soak your reed. After gathering the reed you'll need for a project, preparation of the reed is necessary.

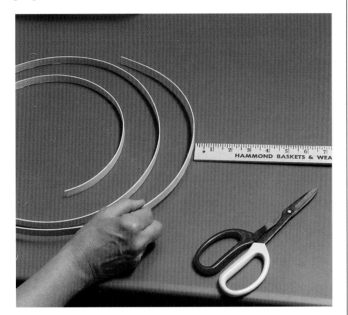

**1.** To get started, cut the bands from a hank of reed.

Leave the end band on to keep the reeds together.

**2.** To prevent tangling, pull out a reed from the far end of the hank, farthest from the band that you left intact.

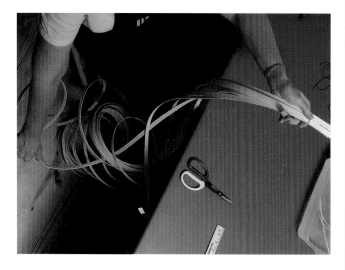

For most projects, you'll need to measure and cut reed that will be used as "spokes," the reeds around which other reeds are woven.

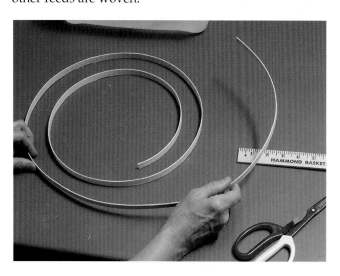

**3.** Measure the spokes using a yardstick. In this case, 22-inch spokes are being measured.

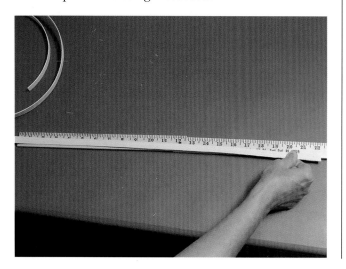

**4.** Cut the spokes to the proper length with craft scissors.

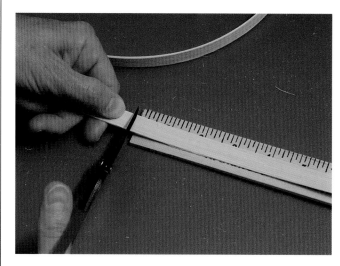

**5.** Fill a plastic pan with warm water. All reed must be soaked before using to keep it pliable and to help prevent it from breaking.

**6.** These spokes have been measured and cut and are soaking in the warm water for several minutes until they are flexible. Reed should soak for five to ten minutes or until it can easily be bent without cracking. Flat oval reed typically must soak longer to become pliable. Cold water can be used, but warm water is more comfortable for the weaver and softens the reeds more quickly.

**7.** Dyed reeds should be soaked for no more than a minute or two and should be dried quickly with a towel to take off excess water so the color doesn't bleed.

**8.** A whole piece of reed is used for weaving. Pull out a reed from the far end of the roll and soak the entire piece before beginning to weave.

**9.** Clothespins can be used to hold pieces of reed together while they soak. It helps them fit in the container better and keeps long reeds from getting tangled. Pinning spokes together can help keep you organized.

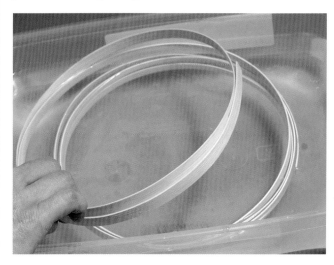

**10.** Reed has a smooth side and a rough side. Many people can tell by feeling the reed between their fingers which side is smoother. Another way to tell is by bending the reed after it has been soaked. Fibers can be seen on the rough side of the reed. Place the smooth side of the reed on the outside of the basket with the rough side facing the inside of the basket.

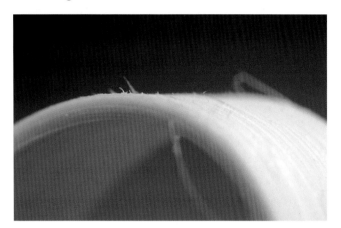

# Part II

## Basic Techniques

# 1

# Flared Bun Basket

The flared bun basket uses natural and dyed reeds. A reed bow accents the completed basket.

**GETTING STARTED**
Materials needed to make the bun basket include:

½" flat reed for spokes, weaving, and rim

½" dyed flat reed for spokes and weaving

#2 round reed for twining

⅜" flat reed for weaving the sides

¼" flat oval reed for weaving and for lashing the rim

#3 seagrass for the rim filler

**1.** Make eight spokes from ½" flat reed. Measure each spoke to 22 inches and cut with your craft scissors.

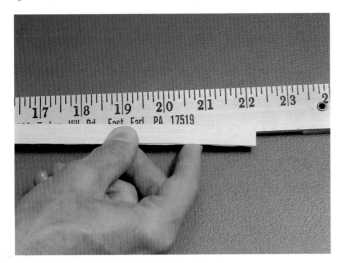

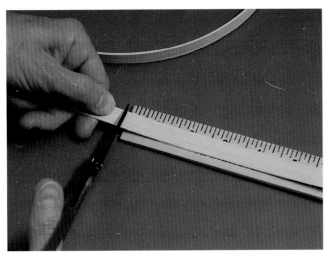

**2.** Cut two additional spokes, also 22 inches long, from dyed reed.

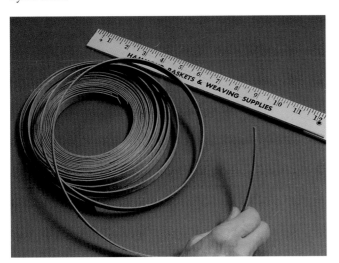

**3.** Soak the eight natural spokes and two dyed spokes.

**4.** Use scissors to cut two pieces of #2 round reed, making each 48 inches long, and soak them in the warm water.

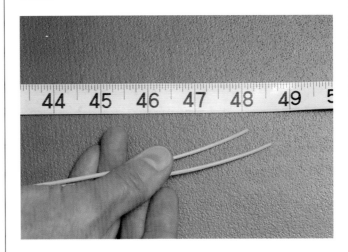

**5.** Remove the spokes from the water and use a pencil to mark the center of each on the rough side. For our 22-inch spokes, the center is at 11 inches.

**Flared Bun Basket**

**6.** After measuring and marking the first spoke, the center of the other spokes can be marked by using the first as a guide. Mark the center of the dyed spokes as well as the natural spokes.

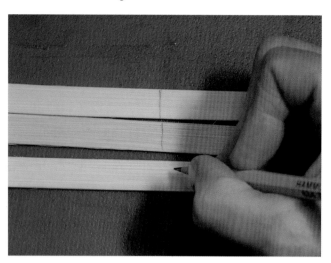

## Weaving Spokes Together

**1.** Now you're ready to begin weaving. With the smooth side down, lay out two natural spokes, one dyed spoke, and two more natural spokes, as shown. Line up the center pencil marks.

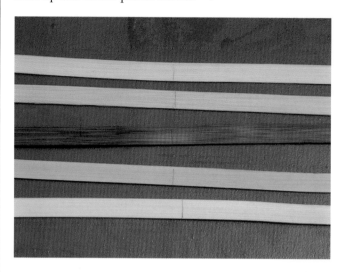

**2.** Take your remaining dyed spoke and weave it in at the center mark.

**3.** Weave over, under, over, under, and over.

**4.** Line up the woven spoke at the center pencil marks. Make sure the center of the woven spoke is over the center dyed spoke.

**5.** Now take a natural spoke and weave to the right side of the dyed spoke, under first this time, then over, under, over, and under, lining up the pencil mark on the weaver under the center dyed reed. Try to keep the spacing even between the spokes. When all spokes are woven, you'll measure and readjust as needed.

After the first two spokes are woven, your basket should look like this.

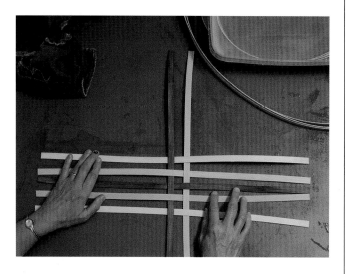

**6.** Weave another natural spoke to the right side of the previous reed: over first, then under, over, under, and over—the same as the dyed spoke.

**7.** Line up the pencil mark at the center.

**8.** Weave a natural spoke to the left of the dyed spoke: under, over, under, over, and under..

**9.** Weave another natural spoke to the left side of the dyed spoke.

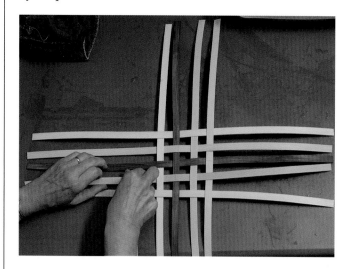

Work the spoke over first, then under.

The base of your basket is nearly complete.

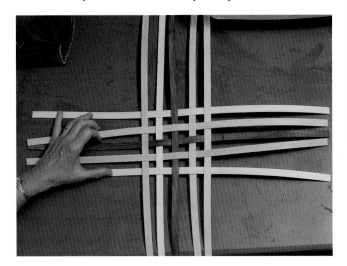

**10.** Measure and adjust the base so that it is 5½ inches wide from the outer edge of the far left spoke to the outer edge of the far right spoke.

**11.** Adjust the spokes until they are all equally separated from each other. Careful measuring and adjusting will help make the finished basket neat and sturdy.

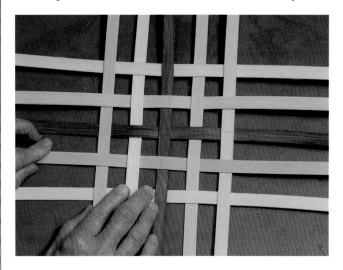

**12.** The base also should be adjusted so it measures 5½ inches high with the reeds evenly spaced. The outer edge of the top spoke should be 5½ inches from the outer edge of the bottom spoke.

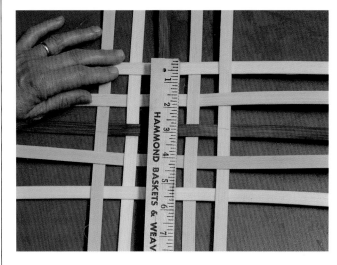

The next step is called twining and it holds the base in place. In this step, two round reeds will not only be woven between the spokes, they will also twine around each other. To accomplish this, you must alternate weaving over and under with one reed then switching to the other reed and weaving over and under with it.

**1.** Take out the two pieces of round reed that have been soaking.

**2.** Start on a side in which the dyed spoke is woven over (not under) the natural spoke at the top edge.

**3.** Slide the first round weaver underneath the natural spoke to the right of the dyed spoke and then over the dyed spoke. You might need to hold the spokes in place as you weave.

**4.** Start the second round weaver on top of the natural spoke to the right of the dyed spoke.

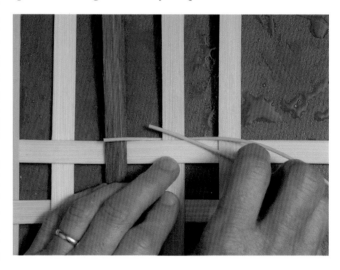

**5.** Keeping the first weaver out of the way to the inside, pull the second round weaver under the end spoke and bend it around the corner where it will be on top of the horizontal spoke. Once the weaver is around the corner, pull it tight.

**6.** Take the first weaver and weave it over the end spoke on the first side, then bend it around the corner and under the horizontal spoke.

**7.** Continue to alternate as you work downwards. Take the second weaver and keep it over the corner spoke, then weave it under the next spoke. Make sure to keep the other weaver to the inside.

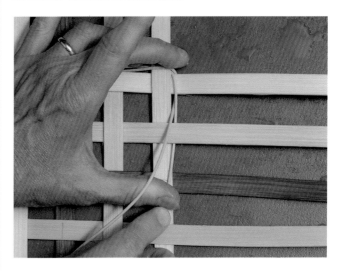

You will need to hold your twining in place with your finger while you continue to weave with the round reeds.

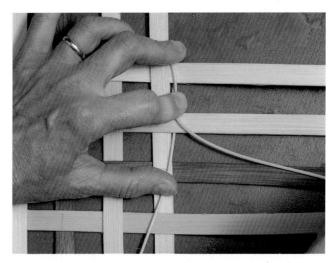

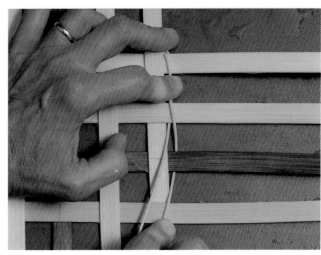

**8.** Continue to switch weavers, weaving over and under with each, keeping the reed not being used to the inside.

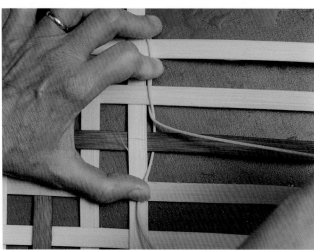

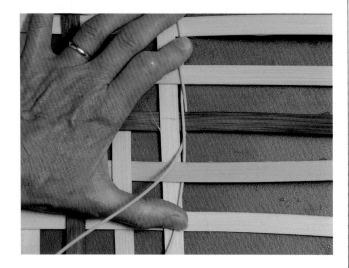

After you've woven around all five horizontal spokes, the twining pattern emerges.

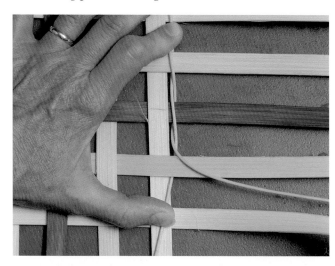

At corners where the end vertical spoke goes over the end horizontal spoke, the weaver can slide under the vertical spoke. To prevent this, we'll use a basket weaver's trick.

**9.** Weave first with the weaver that goes over the vertical spoke. Weave it around the corner and under the horizontal spoke.

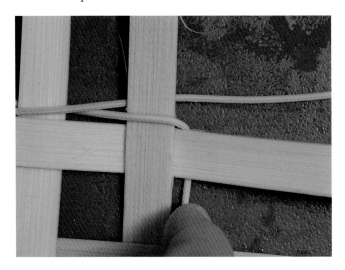

**10.** Now go back to the other weaver, which can be woven under the vertical spoke without sliding beneath it and over the horizontal spoke on the next side.

**11.** Continue twining around the basket until you return to the start. Catch the tail of the first weaver between the weavers.

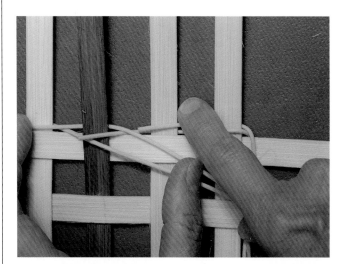

**12.** Catch the end of the second weaver in the same way.

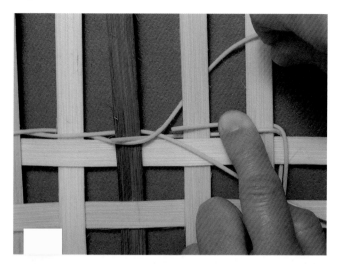

**13.** Continue twining a second time around the base.

If you reverse the order of the two weavers, the two middle weavers will be together instead of alternating.

The twined weavers alternate and are not together.

**14.** Weavers end on the spoke where they began. Once you reach the starting spokes after the second row of twining, clip the ends of your weavers, leaving about 3 inches extra to turn under.

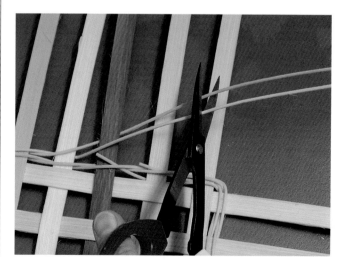

**15.** Wet your fingers, then moisten the ends of the weavers if they have dried.

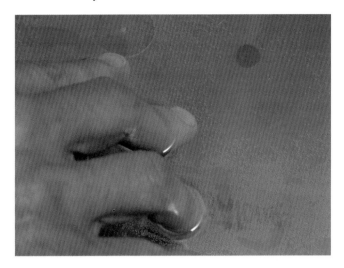

**16.** Use the packing tool to loosen the weaving reed that overlaps the spoke at the first weaver's starting point so you can slide the first weaver under it.

**17.** Pull the first weaver tight.

**18.** Pull the second weaver under the weaver at its starting point as well, using a packing tool if necessary.

**19.** Pull the weavers tight and trim the ends on a diagonal, leaving about ¼ inch behind so each is well secured. The initial ends can be trimmed as well.

Now the base of your basket is secured with twining. It's time to weave the sides.

**1.** You'll need to wet the base of the basket again. It can be plunged into the container of water as shown here. It could also be dampened using a sponge or a spray bottle. If the reeds are still damp, they can be re-moistened quickly. If they've been left to dry completely, they will need to soak for a few minutes. The reeds must be pliable to keep them from cracking during the next step. If a reed cracks but doesn't break in half, it can be sanded smooth when it dries. If a reed breaks, it must be replaced by cutting a new spoke and weaving it into place, being careful to weave correctly through the twining.

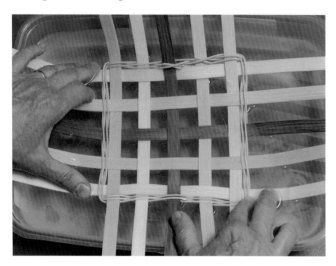

**2.** After the reeds are pliable, bend all the spoke reeds along the edge of the twining so they can form the spokes of the basket.

**3.** Starting at one corner, fold the reed over and pull it tight to the twining. Then crease it down to make it flexible.

**4.** Repeat with each reed. They will fall back into place, but the crease will remain. Now the reeds can be woven into an upright position to form the basket's sides.

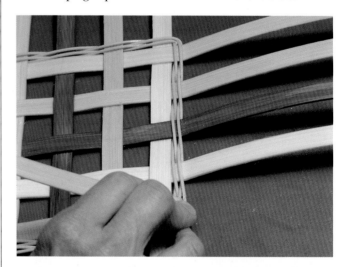

The sides of the basket will be formed with a length of ⅜" flat reed.

**5.** Pull a reed from the roll and soak it in the tub of water for about five minutes or until it's flexible.

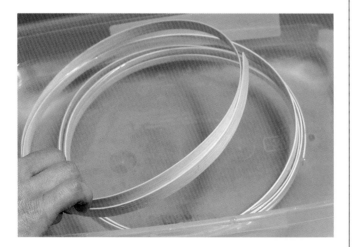

With this basket, start each weave on the outside of the second spoke from the corner. By starting on the second spoke, enough room is left to overlap each weaver. Use the smooth side of the reed on the outside of the basket with the rough side facing inside the basket. Make sure the first row weaves alternately from the base.

If you don't, instead of alternating, the base and side weavers will be side by side. Both go over the dyed reed, as shown here.

Find a side where starting on the second spoke makes the side weaver alternate with the base. The base weaver goes under the dyed reed and the side weaver goes over the dyed reed.

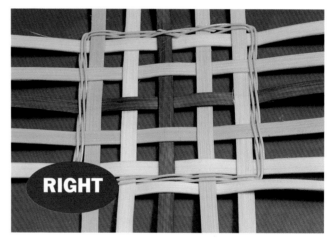

**6.** Use a clothespin to attach the first weaver to the outside of the spoke and weave it under and over to the corner.

**7.** Carefully bend the weaver around the corner and pin it to secure it in place.

**8.** Continue weaving and pinning the weaver to each corner.

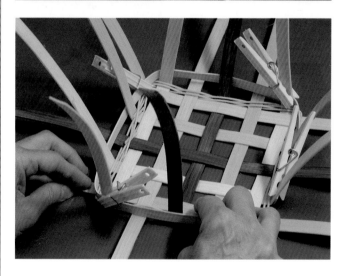

**9.** Once you get back to the starting point of the first weaver, remove the clothespin and replace it over both thicknesses of the weaver.

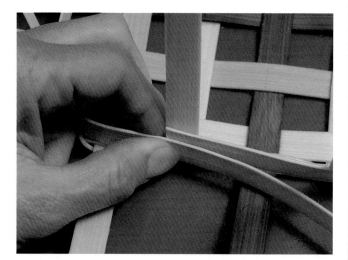

**10.** Overlap the weaver to the fourth spoke and cut the weaver so that it will be hidden underneath the spoke (bent down here, underneath the scissors).

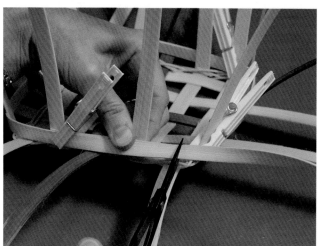

The first weaver is hidden under the fourth spoke on the left of this photo. The second row of weaving will begin around the corner from where the first weaver ends.

**11.** On this basket, each weaver begins in front of the second spoke from the left. Start the second row of weaving by pinning the weaver to the second spoke so it faces out.

**12.** The second row of weaving alternates with the first row of weaving. Make sure to keep the rough side of the reed toward the inside of the basket. Continue to weave around the basket, gently bending the weavers around the corners and pinning in place. By the time the second row of weaving is done, the spokes will stand upright.

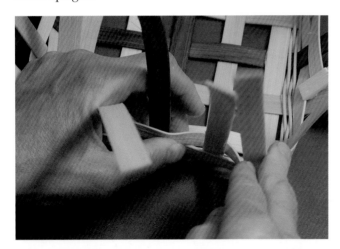

**13.** Again, overlap the second row of weaving by continuing to weave four spokes past the beginning of the weave.

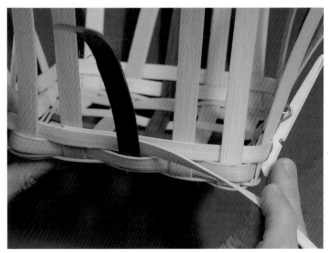

**14.** Cut the end of the second weaver so it is hidden behind the fourth spoke, past the spoke where it began.

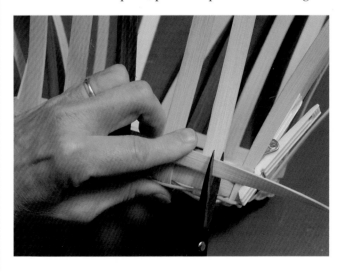

The cut weaver goes behind the spokes.

**15.** Every time you start a new row, turn the basket to the next side. Begin the third row of weaving on the second spoke from the left. Remember that each weaver must alternate with the weaver beneath it. End by overlapping four spokes, cutting the weaver and hiding it behind a spoke.

**16.** As you weave, keep the rows packed down tight by pressing them with your fingers.

**17.** Adjust the spokes from time to time so they are evenly spaced and straight.

After weaving the first three rows of ⅜" flat reed, you'll use ¼" flat oval reed to weave seven more rows.

The oval side of the reed always faces out.

**18.** Soak the oval reed for five to ten minutes until it's flexible and use the same starting and stopping techniques as with the flat reed.

**19.** Start by turning the basket to the next side from where the last row of flat reed ended.

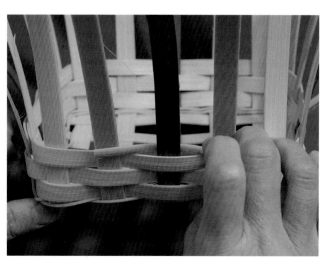

**20.** Pin the flat oval weaver to the outside of the second spoke from the left and begin to weave.

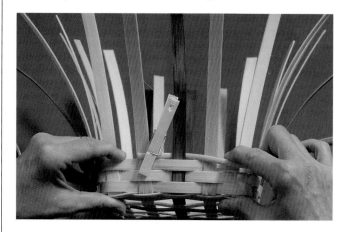

**21.** The shaping technique changes with these seven rows. The center spoke on each side of the basket will stay straight, but the other spokes will be gently fanned so that the basket will flare slightly. When you weave to the corner, hold the spoke in position and weave to the other side.

**22.** After you weave through the corner, pull back on the weaver slightly to relieve the tension at each corner. By pulling back the weaver at each corner, you will slightly lengthen each row of weaving. This is what causes the flaring.

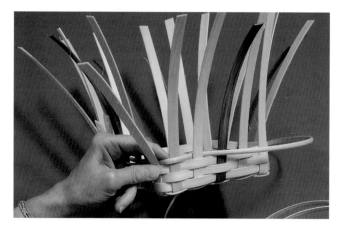

**23.** Adjust and shift spokes as needed to keep them uniformly spaced.

**24.** Just as with the flat reed, overlap the end of the flat oval weaver by four spokes, cut the weaver, and hide it behind the fourth spoke.

**25.** Add seven rows of flat oval reeds, adjusting the tension at the corners to allow for gentle flaring and keeping the spokes evenly spaced.

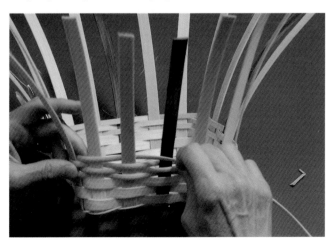

See how this basket is beginning to flare. Remember to keep the rows of weaving packed down tight.

By the time seven rows of flat oval weavers are added, your basket should look like this. The seventh flat oval weaver is cut so it can be tucked behind the fourth overlap spoke.

**26.** One row of dyed ½" flat reed is added for accent. Just as with other weavers, clip it to the front of the second spoke from the left, making sure the weaving alternates with the row of flat oval weaving below.

**27.** Weave back to the beginning and overlap by four spokes.

**28.** Turn the basket to the next side and begin weaving three more rows of ⅜" flat weavers, continuing to flare the basket as you go.

**29.** After the final three rows of weaving have been completed, pack down each row of weaving with a packing tool, starting at the bottom of the basket. This step helps keep a tight basket because reeds shrink as they dry. Push each row of weaving down with the packing tool.

**30.** Once the basket has been packed, wet the tops of the spokes by dipping them into the pan of water.

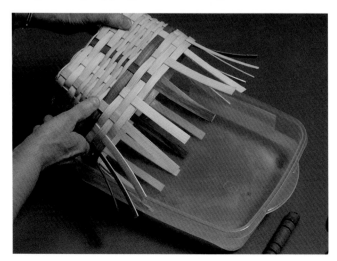

**31.** Beginning with a dyed spoke on the outside of the top weaver, cut it on a diagonal about 2½ inches from the top of the weaver.

**32.** Fold it down tight.

**33.** Weave it through about three reeds on the inside of the basket, using the packing tool if needed.

**34.** Repeat with every other spoke: the ones that are on the outside of the top row of weaving.

**35.** Cut off the rest of the spokes inside the top row of weaving so they are flush with the top of the basket.

**1.** Measure the lashing needed for the basket rim by wrapping it around the basket three times. Cut off the excess. Use the same ¼" flat oval reed for the lashing that was used for weaving. Soak the reed for five to ten minutes to make it pliable. By the time you're ready to use it, it should be pliable.

**2.** The rim of the basket will be made using an inside and outside row of ½" flat reed with twisted #3 seagrass used as an accent to fill in between the rims. Wind the seagrass once around the basket and cut it 3 to 4 inches longer. The flat reed used for the rim needs to be soaked; the seagrass does not.

**3.** Begin by pinning the outside of the ½" flat reed to the top of the basket near a corner, keeping the smooth side of the rim material to the outside.

**4.** Pin the rim material all the way around the top of the basket.

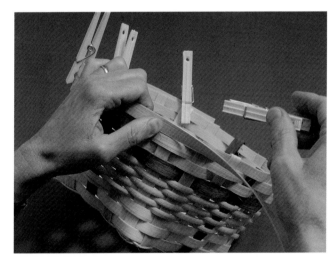

When you get back to the beginning, pin the rim material to overlap by about four spokes and cut.

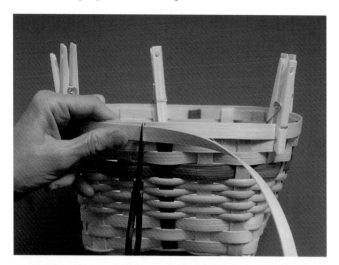

**5.** Use the same procedure with the inside of the rim, beginning the rim material where the overlap of the outside rim ends. Pin it in place and keep the smooth side facing out (toward the inside of the basket).

**6.** Continue pinning the inside rim material in place and overlap it by about four spokes as well before cutting it.

**7.** Starting near the end of the outside rim material, begin to pin the seagrass in place between the inside and outside rim. Carefully remove the pins holding the rim material in place to add the seagrass, then replace the pins.

## Securing Lashers with a Fishhook

**1.** Soak a piece of ¼" flat oval reed to use as a lasher. Begin lashing the rim together past the rim overlaps. Use the "fishhook" technique to lock your ¼" flat oval lasher in place. A fishhook starts on the inside of the basket and ends on the outside. With the oval side of the lasher facing the inside of the basket, push it up between the inside rim and the basket, coming out between the seagrass and the outside rim of the basket. Pull up about 3 inches of lasher.

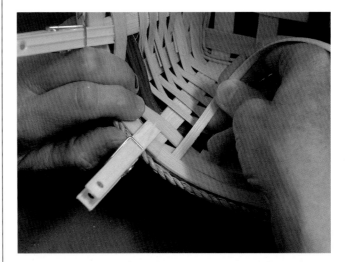

**8.** When you've reached the starting point of the seagrass, cut it to overlap by about an inch or two.

**2.** Now fold back the lasher and insert it in the same space between the seagrass and the outer rim but to the outside of the top row of weaving on the basket.

**3.** Pull the lasher down tight to lock. Your fishhook is in place. Now you can begin to lash the basket rim.

**4.** Bring the long end of the lasher up and over the rim of the basket, pulling it tight and pinning to keep secure.

**5.** Making sure the lasher is not twisted, insert it between the next two spokes using the packing tool.

**6.** Pull it through and tighten.

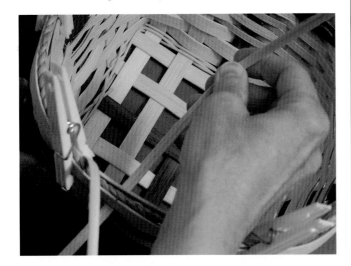

**7.** Use the packing tool to insert the lasher in the space between the next two spokes, again making sure the lasher is not twisted.

**8.** Continue lashing between each spoke, keeping lashes as even as you can.

**9.** When you reach the overlap area, squeeze it closed with the lashing as tightly as possible.

**10.** Cut the end of the outside rim on a diagonal about ¼ to ⅜ inch beyond one of the lashings.

**11.** To hide the ends of the seagrass, cut both ends so the seagrass meets under the lash. Make sure you know where the lash will fall before you cut the seagrass.

**12.** Butt the ends of the seagrass together so they are covered by the lash.

**13.** Continue lashing until you reach the end of the inside rim.

**14.** Just like the outside rim, cut the inside rim on a diagonal next to a lashing.

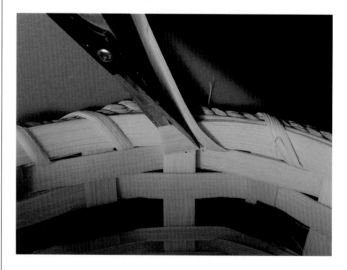

**15.** The last lash is inserted beside the fishhook tail.

**16.** Pull it tight.

**17.** Fasten the final lashing the same way the fishhook was initially begun, starting on the inside and ending on the outside.

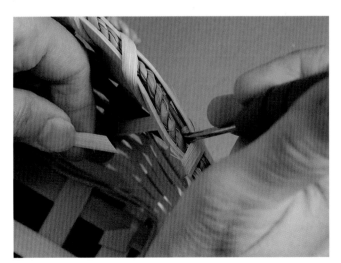

Using the packing tool, slide the lasher from inside the basket between the seagrass and the outside rim of the basket.

**18.** Pull up the lasher tight.

**19.** Insert the lasher down between the seagrass and outside rim and the outside of the basket.

**20.** Pull it tight next to the initial fishhook. Trim both ends flush with the bottom of the rim.

## Adding a Decorative Bow

**1.** A decorative bow can be added to the basket by using a 34-inch piece of dyed ½" flat reed. Soak the reed for a minute or two and dry off excess water with your towel.

**2.** Clip off the corners of the reed so it weaves through easier.

**3.** Choose a side of the basket where the vertical dyed spoke is on the outside of the horizontal dyed weaver. With the rough side facing out, slide the 34-inch reed behind the dyed spoke and pull it so that half of the reed is on each side.

**4.** Bring up one end of the reed and weave it back under the same spoke.

**5.** Pull it to make a small loop.

**6.** Bring up the other tail and, using the packing tool, weave it behind the same spoke. Make another small loop.

**7.** Adjust the reeds to make the loops the same size.

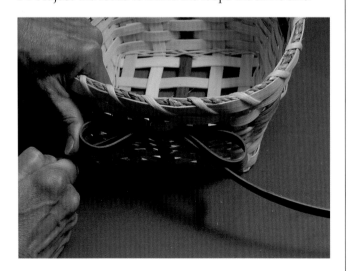

**8.** Take the ends and curve them down, inserting under the second weaver on the corner spoke.

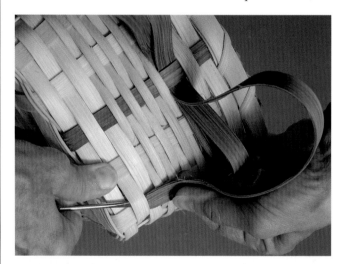

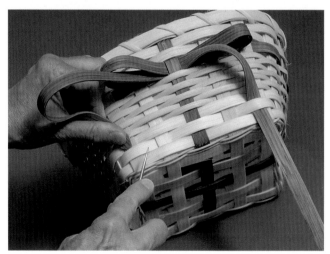

**9.** When adjusted the way you like, cut off the ends diagonally so they are no longer than the basket.

## Finishing a Basket

You may want to finish your basket by trimming fibers that protrude from it. This would apply to any basket you make.

Add your initials or name and the date to the bottom of the basket.

# 2

# Small Market Basket

The small market basket has a closed woven base and uses dyed flat weavers that form a chain design.

**GETTING STARTED**
Materials needed to complete the small market basket include:

⅝" flat reed for spokes and the rim
½" flat reed for base fillers
#2 round reed: two pieces, each 8½ feet long
6" by 10" D handle
⅜" flat reed for weaving
⅜" dyed flat reed for weaving
¼" flat reed for lashing the rim
#3 seagrass for the rim

Many of the steps in making the market basket are similar to the steps already explained in making the flared bun basket. Please refer to those directions if you have questions about these particular steps.

**1.** Cut eleven spokes from ⅝" flat reed. Cut five spokes 24 inches long and six spokes 22 inches long. Use a pencil to mark each at the center, 12 inches for the longer spokes and 11 inches for the shorter spokes.

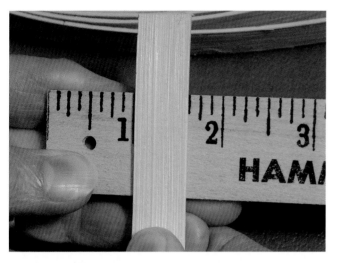

**2.** Cut four fillers, each 16 inches long, from ½" flat reed. Mark their centers at 8 inches. Use two pieces of #2 round reed that are 8½ feet long.

**3.** Using four clothespins, pin together the 24-inch spokes, the 22-inch spokes, the fillers, and the round reed. Soak them in a container of warm water for several minutes until they are pliable.

**4.** Use your yardstick to mark the center of the base of the 6" by 10" D handle with a pencil. The center will be at 3 inches.

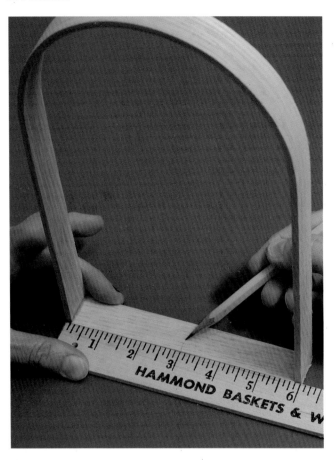

**5.** Remove the five longer spokes and the four fillers from the water. Lay them out smooth side down, alternating the fillers between the long spokes and lining up the pencil marks at the centers.

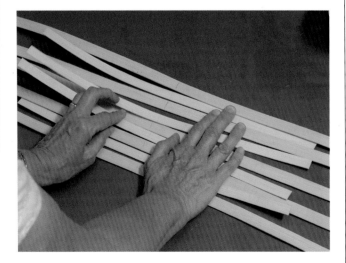

## Adding a Handle

**1.** Next, weave in the handle so the short fillers are on top and the long spokes on the bottom.

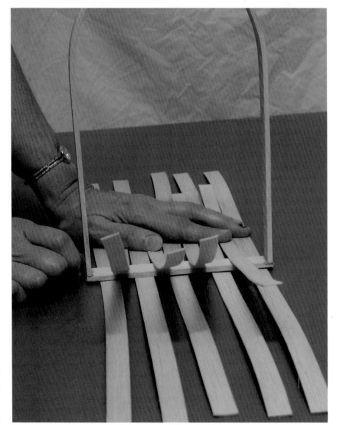

**2.** Line up the center marks on the fillers and spokes along the center of the width of the handle. Keep the mark on the handle in the center of the width of the middle spoke.

**3.** Take the remaining spokes and weave the first to the right of the handle. Treat the handle as a spoke and begin weaving the first spoke under then over.

**4.** Line up the center line on the weaver with the center spoke. Push the weaver within ⅜ inch of the handle.

**5.** Weave two more spokes on the right side of the handle, as shown.

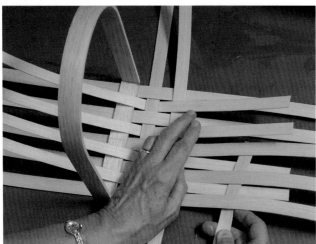

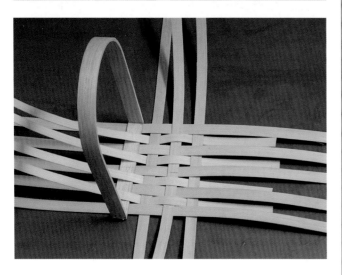

**6.** Now weave three spokes to the left side of the handle, beginning next to the handle and remembering to start the first weaver under then over.

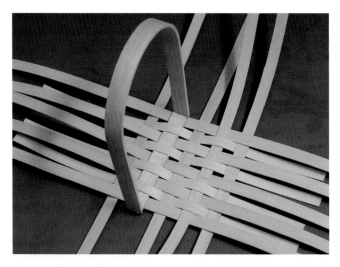

Now your basket should look like this.

**7.** Measure an 8-inch length on the bottom of the basket by putting the ruler so that the 4-inch line is at the center of the handle.

**8.** Adjust the end spokes so that the outside edge of the one is at the beginning of the ruler and the outside edge of the other is at the 8-inch line.

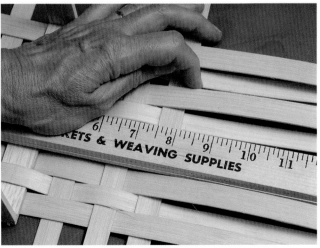

**9.** Adjust the remaining two spokes on each side so they are evenly spaced.

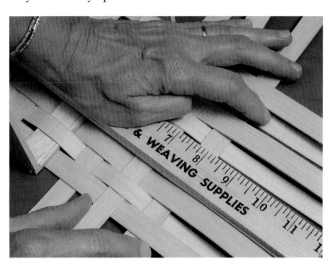

**10.** Pack the lengthwise spokes toward the center spoke using the packing tool.

When all spokes are packed, the basket bottom should look like this.

**11.** Wet the edge of the basket either by dipping it in the pan of water or by using your fingers, a sponge, or a spray bottle.

**12.** While the edge is still wet, fold up the fillers tight against the end spokes.

**13.** Cut off on the diagonal at the third spoke.

**14.** Slide the filler under the third spoke, using the packing tool if necessary.

The end of the filler is hidden by the spoke.

Make sure no cut ends show.

**15.** Continue the same procedure with the remainder of the fillers.

**16.** After the fillers are in place, pack the lengthwise spokes tightly in to the center spoke again.

**17.** Take water-soaked #2 round reeds and start twining to fill in the space at the base of the handle. About three rows of twining using #2 round reed will be needed.

**18.** Start on one end of the basket. Begin one twining reed on top of the second spoke and start the next twining reed on top of the third spoke.

**19.** Weave under and over with one reed then under and over with the other reed, keeping the reed not being used to the inside.

**20.** At the corners, use the twining techniques as were demonstrated for the flared bun basket.

**21.** At the handle, make sure your upper reed is out of the way while you weave the lower reed underneath the basket handle. Treat the handle as if it were another spoke.

**22.** Keep weaving about two spokes at a time with each weaver, bringing the reed you're weaving with to the outside so it crosses the other weaver, then pulling it to the inside on the next spoke, forming the twining pattern.

**23.** On the opposite side, keep the upper reed out of the way while you weave the lower reed underneath the basket handle.

**24.** Once you reach the starting point, catch the tails of the weavers from the inside.

**25.** The first tail is caught. Now catch the second tail.

**26.** Continue twining two more rows, making sure the twining alternates.

Remember to keep the upper reed out of the way while you weave the lower reed under the basket handle.

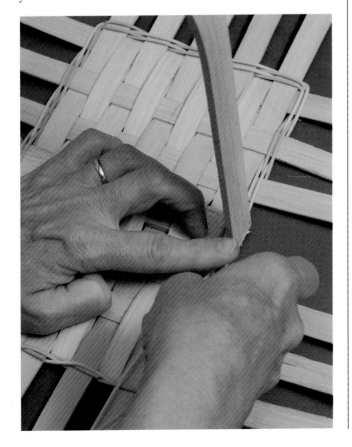

Notice how the twining alternates.

**27.** End where you started, leaving about 3 inches of reed. Twining reeds can be trimmed off on the diagonal or tucked under.

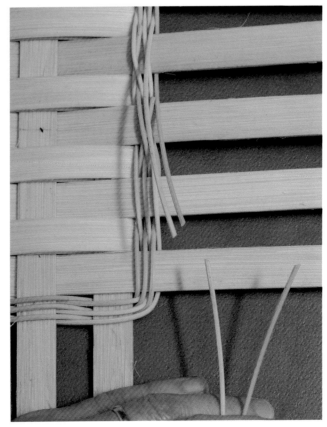

**28.** To tuck them, use your packing tool to create space so the reed can slide under the two rows of twining.

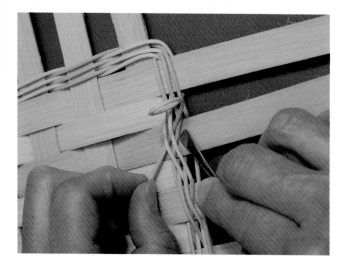

**29.** Repeat with both reeds and pull tight.

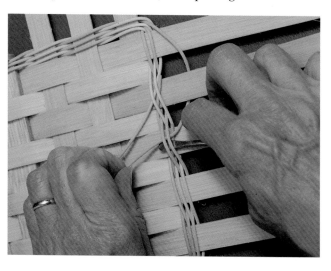

**30.** Snip both ends on a diagonal close to the twining.

**1.** Wet the spokes at the edges of the basket bottom so they can be folded.

**2.** Beginning at one corner, bend over each spoke tight to the edge . . .

. . . and fold it over.

**3.** Continue bending and folding each spoke.

**4.** Next, begin creating the sides of the basket. Soak a strand of ⅜" flat reed for several minutes until it is flexible. The first weaver will be woven outside the handle and will begin on the long side of the basket. Start on the outside of the second spoke from the left and clip the weaver to the spoke.

**5.** Weave over and under the spokes, remembering to weave around the handle as if it were another spoke. Keep the first row of weaving tight to the twining.

**6.** Make a sharp corner and pin it in place.

**7.** Continue weaving and making sharp corners, pinning in place after each corner.

**8.** When you reach the beginning of the weave, overlap the weaver by four spokes.

**9.** Cut off the weaver just inside the fourth spoke so that it will be hidden behind the spoke.

**10.** Pin it behind the spoke to hold it in place.

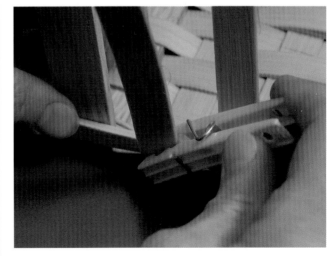

**11.** Turn the basket to the next side and pin the flat reed weaver to the outside of the second spoke from the left.

**12.** Weave over and under and bend the weaver squarely at every corner.

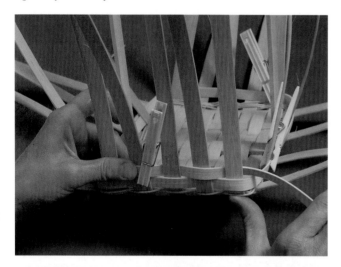

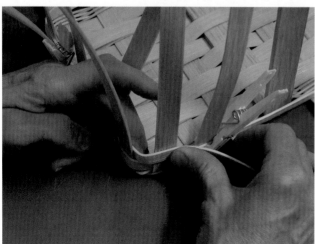

**13.** Weave behind the handle with the second weaver. Keep the spokes evenly spaced.

**14.** When you get back to the beginning, overlap the weaver by four spokes. Cut and hide the end of the weaver behind the fourth spoke. Make sure the first row overlap stays in place.

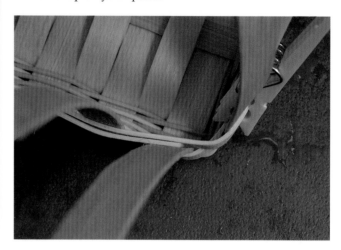

**15.** Turn your basket to the next side and start your third row of weaving as before on the outside of the second spoke.

As you continue to weave, make sure the corner spokes come up straight. Sometimes they bend in, causing the basket to get smaller as you weave.

**16.** Adjust and pull in the corners as you continue to weave to keep the basket straight.

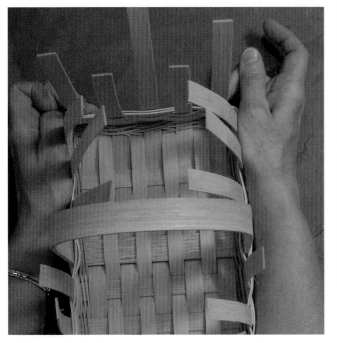

**17.** Weave five rows of the ⅜" natural flat reed.

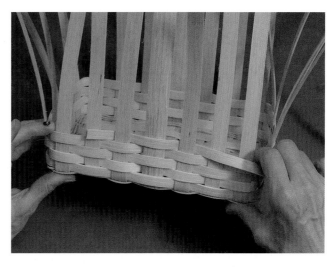

**18.** Keep each row of weavers as close as possible to the row beneath it.

## Adding a Chain Design with Dyed Reed

**1.** Add three rows of dyed reeds in your choice of color. Soak a strand of ⅜" dyed flat reed for a minute or two.

**2.** Wipe off the excess water with a towel so the color doesn't bleed.

**3.** Start your first dyed reed on the outside of the second spoke at the end of the basket.

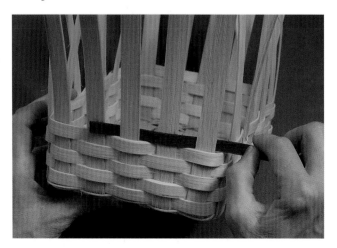

**4.** Weave the same as before, overlapping by four spokes and hiding the end of the weaver behind the fourth spoke.

The end of the weaver is hidden behind the fourth spoke.

**5.** Remember to start each new row on the next side of the basket from where you finish the previous weaver.

By the time you weave the third row of dyed reed into the basket, a chain pattern emerges.

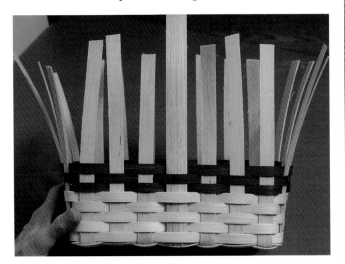

**6.** Next, add three more rows of ⅜" natural flat reed, turning the basket to the next side to add each row.

**7.** Continue to adjust the basket to keep the corners square. Make sure the spokes are evenly spaced.

**8.** Once you weave the third and final row of natural flat reed, use your packing tool to pack the weavers tight toward the base of the basket to prevent gaps. Begin at the bottom row of weaving and work upward. For a tighter basket, you can let the basket dry for a few hours or overnight and then pack it. If you allow the reeds to dry completely, be sure to wet the ends of the spokes thoroughly before the next step to prevent cracking.

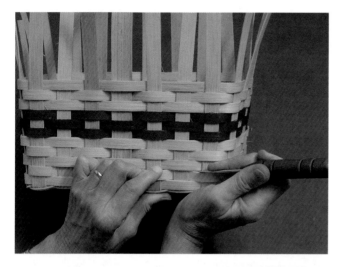

## Finishing the Basket Sides

**1.** After packing each row of weavers, wet the tops of the spokes in preparation for folding.

**2.** Fold in every other spoke (the spokes that are on the outside of the top row of weaving).

**3.** Cut off each folded spoke on the diagonal so they can be tucked under two weavers on the inside of the basket.

**4.** Because cutting off the spokes inside the basket can be tricky, you can make a template from a scrap piece of reed that you can use to measure and cut the rest of the spokes while they stand upright.

65

Spokes should be tucked behind both inside weavers. Use the packing tool if necessary. This folded spoke missed the top weaver.

This spoke has been correctly tucked behind the top and second inside weaver.

**5.** Continue to fold and tuck all the outside spokes to the inside of the basket.

**6.** After you tuck in all the outside spokes, trim the inside spokes even with the top of the basket.

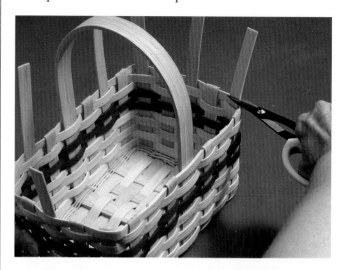

The rim on this basket will be finished similarly to the flared bun basket. Check rim instructions for that basket before proceeding.

**1.** Measure the lashing needed for the basket rim by wrapping ¼" flat reed around the basket three times.

**2.** Wrap seagrass around the basket one time to measure and add a few inches overlap before cutting. Soak the lashing and one strand of ⅝" flat reed rim material, but not the seagrass.

**3.** Pin the rough sides of the ⅝" flat reed rim material against the basket. Start the outside rim close to the corner and pin it on the top row of weaving.

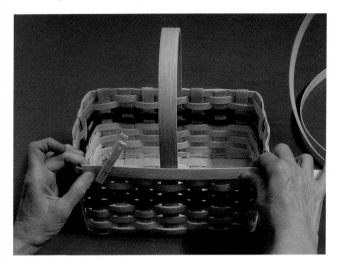

**4.** Shape the corners as you go so you don't lose the sharp corner.

**5.** End the outside rim before the handle and cut it.

**6.** Start the inside rim at the handle, pinning it and shaping it in the corner.

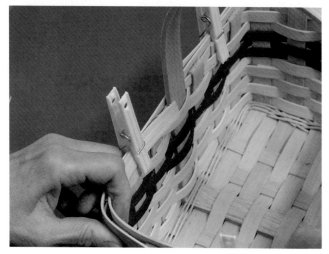

**7.** Continue pinning the inside rim around the basket.

**8.** End the inside rim in the corner past its starting point and cut it.

**9.** Begin inserting the seagrass between the inside and outside rim near the first overlap.

**10.** Place the seagrass to the outside of the handle.

**11.** Pin and place seagrass all the way around the basket, ending with a little overlap.

**12.** Take the ¼" flat reed lashing from the water. Place it at the basket handle on the opposite side of the rim overlaps. Wrap it around the back of the handle with the rough side toward the handle. Half of the length of lashing should be on either side of the handle.

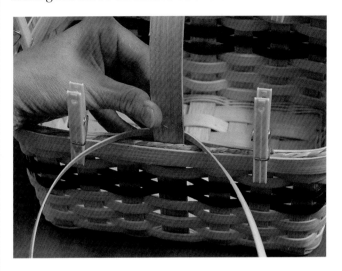

**13.** Pin the lashing in place.

**14.** Bring the lash from the right side of the handle and under the rim on the left side of the handle. You may need your packing tool to do this. Pull the lash tight.

**15.** Now bring the lash from the left side of the handle and insert under the rim on the right side of the handle, making an X. Use your packing tool if necessary.

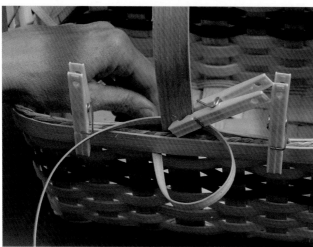

**16.** Keep the left side tightly in place as you work. Pull the right side tight and pin it to hold.

**17.** Begin weaving with the left lash, making sure it is not twisted. Feed it under the rim through the next space between spokes.

**18.** Pull tight.

**19.** Keep lashing to the left between each spoke until you reach the overlap.

**20.** When you reach the overlap, pull the lashing tight and pin it in place.

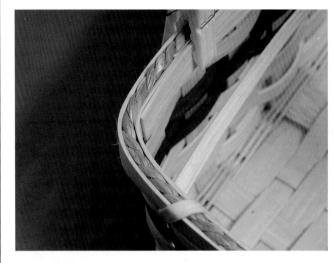

**21.** Now take the lash on the right side of the handle and start lashing to the right. The lashes on opposite sides of the handle will point toward each other.

**22.** Continue lashing around the basket.

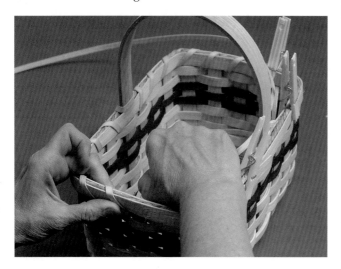

**23.** Keep lashing when you reach the overlap area.

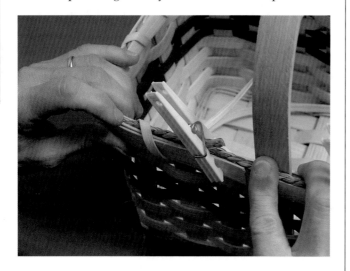

**24.** Cut off the seagrass so it will be hidden under a lash.

**25.** Cut off the end of the rim material on a diagonal.

**26.** The last lash on this side will cross the handle. Insert under the rim and pull tight.

**27.** To hold the end of the lash in place, weave it back through the last two lashes on the inside of the basket.

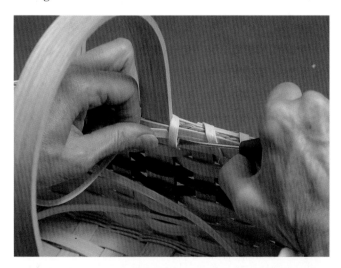

Two lashes will hold it securely.

**28.** Pull the lash tight, keeping it to the bottom of the rim.

**29.** Cut off on a diagonal.

**30.** Now weave the remaining lash the rest of the way around the rim.

Your last lash will make an X on the handle.

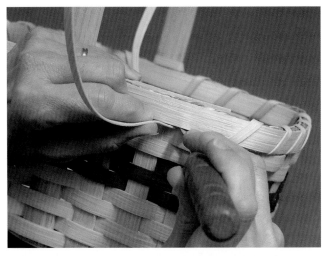

**31.** Finish the same as on the other side by pulling the lash back on itself behind the last two lashes on the inside of the basket.

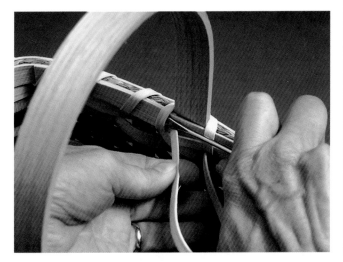

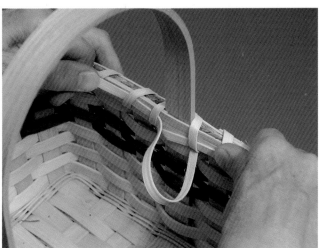

**32.** Cut the lash on the diagonal.

**33.** Shape the corners of the basket, making them square, while the rim is still damp.

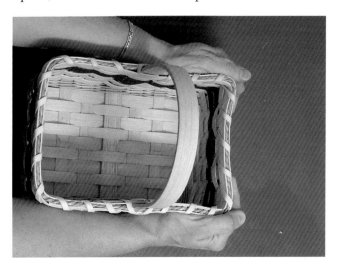

**34.** You've finished your small market basket. Hang it on a hook for a few hours so the bottom of the basket can dry thoroughly.

# 3

# Napkin Basket

This basket uses many of the skills learned in the previous two baskets. In addition, you will learn how to add a decorative triple arrow weave and a diagonal weave to fill in the base of the basket.

## GETTING STARTED
Materials needed to complete this basket include:

- ½" flat reed for the spokes and for the rim
- #2 round reed for twining
- ⅜" flat reed for weaving
- #3 round reed dyed in your choice of color for the triple arrow weaving
- #3 seagrass for the rim
- ¼" flat reed to lash the rim and to use as diagonal base fillers

**1.** To begin, cut fourteen spokes from ½" flat reed, each 18 inches long.

**2.** Soak the spokes in warm water for several minutes until flexible. Mark each in the center on the rough side with a pencil. The center is at 9 inches. Soak two pieces of #2 round reed.

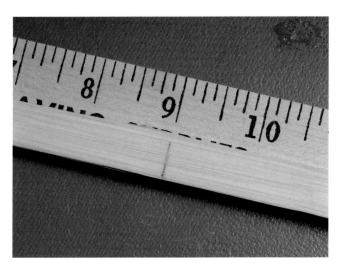

**3.** Take the spokes from the water and lay out seven spokes horizontally.

**4.** Take another spoke and begin weaving over, under, over, under at the center marks on the horizontal spokes.

**5.** Line up the center mark on the weaver under the center spoke.

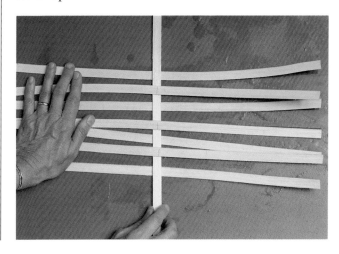

**6.** Weave three more rows of spokes to the right of the spoke you just placed, alternating the weaving. Because you began weaving over with the center spoke, start the next spoke by weaving under.

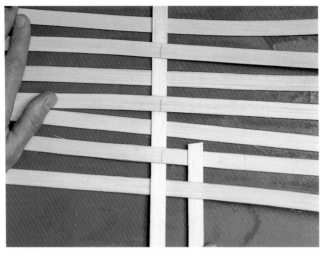

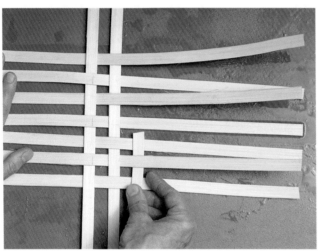

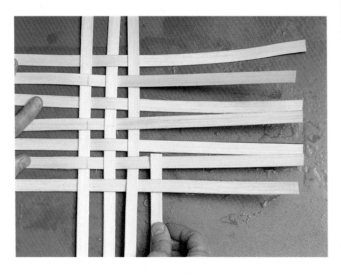

**7.** Once you've woven three spokes to the right of the center spoke, weave three more to the left.

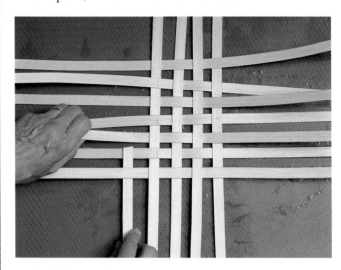

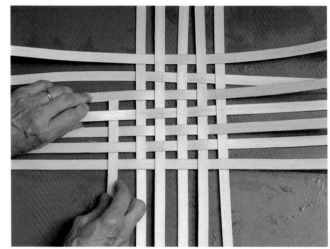

Your basket base should look like this when all fourteen spokes are loosely woven together.

**8.** Now square up the base to 7 inches by lining up the 3½-inch mark on your ruler with the center mark on the center spoke.

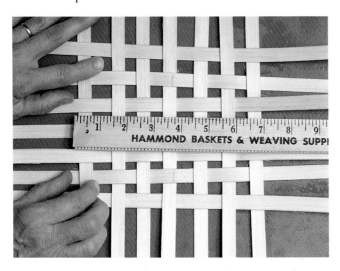

**9.** Pull the outside vertical spokes to line up at the beginning of the ruler and at the 7-inch mark. Adjust the remaining spokes so they are evenly spaced.

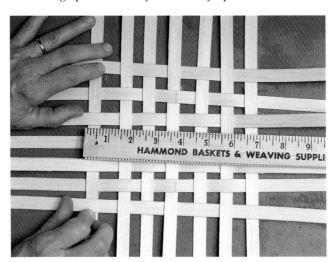

**10.** Do the same with the horizontal spokes, lining up the outside spokes and evenly spacing the remaining spokes.

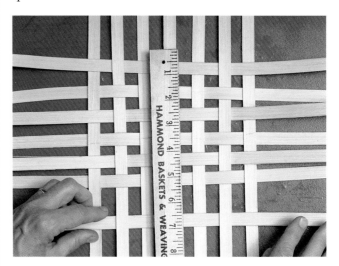

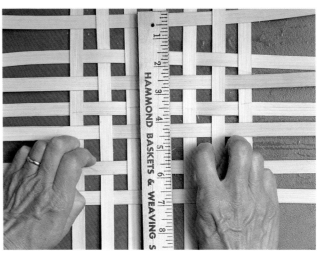

**11.** When you're done adjusting the spokes, check that each edge measures 7 inches.

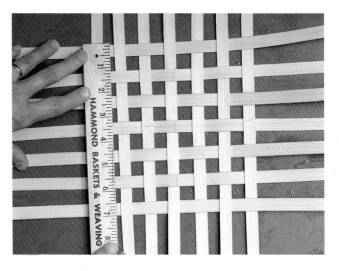

Your base should now look like this.

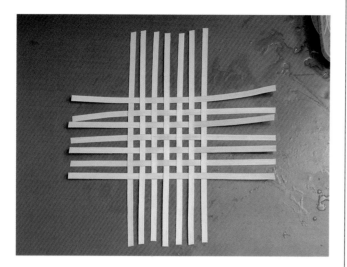

**12.** Take the two pieces of #2 round reed from the container of water. Begin twining by starting the two pieces of reed on top of two consecutive spokes. Continue twining as you did for the flared bun and small market baskets.

**13.** Remember to weave over one spoke and under the next with one weaver before switching to the second weaver.

**14.** Continue to switch weavers and keep the reed you're not weaving to the inside.

**15.** You'll use the basket weaver's trick here again. Because the weaver that goes under the spoke on the corner could slide beneath it, you'll weave with the weaver that goes on top of the spoke first. Weave around the corner and under the next spoke.

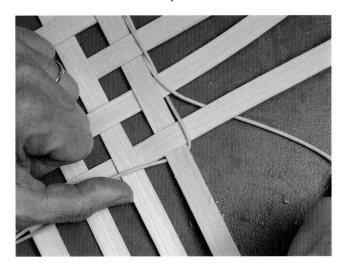

**16.** Now take the second weaver and weave it under the spoke, around the corner, and over the next spoke.

**17.** Weave a second row of twining.

**18.** Once you've woven two rows of twining and are back to the start, clip the ends of your weavers to about 3 inches long.

**19.** Slide the weavers under at the same place where they started.

**20.** Trim beginning and ending tails of the weavers on a diagonal to about ¼ inch.

**21.** Your basket base should now look like this. Soak the spokes at the edges of the basket base before the next step to prevent them from cracking.

**1.** Bend each spoke tight to the twining.

**2.** Fold over each spoke.

**3.** Continue bending and folding spokes all the way around the basket base.

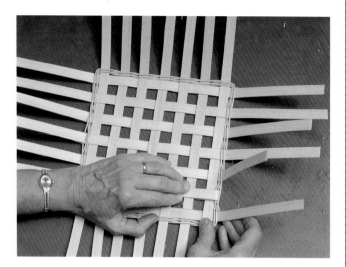

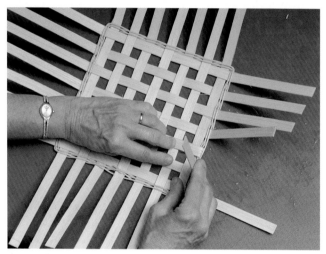

**4.** Begin weaving with a ⅜" flat reed that has been soaked until it is flexible.

**5.** Keep the smooth side of the reed facing out and pin the beginning of the reed in place to a spoke. To leave enough room to overlap your weaver, start on the outside of a spoke at least four spokes from the right corner of the basket. We've started on the second spoke from the left.

**6.** Check that your weaver alternates with the spoke on the base that parallels the weaver.

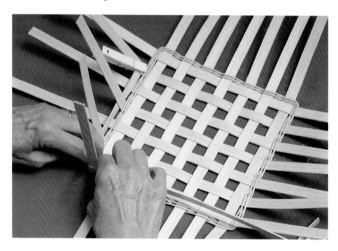

**7.** Keep the bottom row of weaving tight to the base and bend gently at the corner, pinning to hold in place.

**8.** As with previous baskets, overlap the weaver by four spokes, cutting the reed to hide beneath the spoke.

**9.** Turn the basket to the next side and begin your second row of weaving, pinning the weaver in place.

The second row of weaving will bring all of the spokes into an upright position and the third row of weaving will firm up the basket.

**10.** Keep the rows of weaving tight to the base as you go, continuing to overlap each weaver by four spokes. Adjust the spokes as needed to keep them straight up and evenly spaced.

**11.** Always turn the basket to the next side to begin a new row of weaving.

**12.** After the fourth row of weaving is in place, square the basket while it is still damp. As with previous baskets, pack each row of weavers with the packing tool, beginning with the row closest to the base.

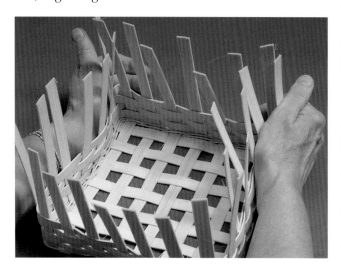

## Using Round Reed to Form a Triple Arrow Weave

**1.** You will need three pieces of #3 dyed round reed. You can measure each reed by wrapping it around your basket twice and adding several extra inches. Soak the reed for a minute or two and dry with a towel to prevent the color from bleeding. Start by placing each piece of reed behind a spoke for three consecutive spokes, as shown below.

**2.** Mark an X at the top of the spoke behind which you've placed the first reed.

**3.** Holding the ends of the three weavers inside the basket with your left hand, start the weave by bringing the weaver farthest to the left in front of two spokes, behind one spoke, and out the next space. Keep the other two weavers on the outside of the basket down and out of the way.

**4.** Repeat with the next weaver farthest to the left, bringing it in front of two spokes and behind one spoke.

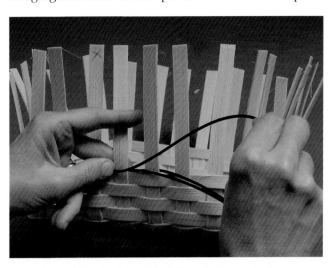

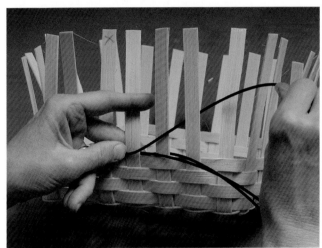

**5.** Begin weaving the third weaver in front of two spokes and behind one.

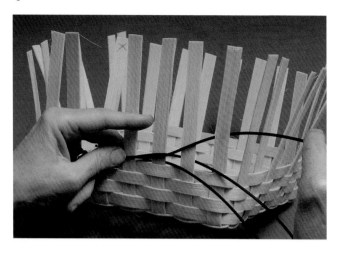

Each space should have one and only one weaver coming out. Make sure you don't have a missed space. Pin the weave in place, as shown.

**6.** Continue with the same pattern of weaving in front of two spokes and behind one spoke, always using the weaver farthest to the left and keeping the other weavers down and out of the way.

**7.** Use your finger to help shape the three weavers around the corner. You need to keep a certain amount of tension on the weavers in the corners and along the sides of the basket to keep them snug and lying smooth. A weaver that is too loose can look bumpy rather than flat.

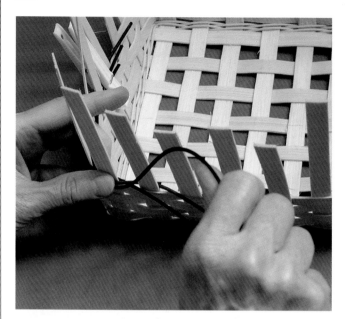

**8.** Continue weaving in the same pattern.

**9.** When you get back to the spoke marked with an X, remove the clothespin. Then you will do a "step up" to form a level ending to the first row of weaving. Instead of beginning with the left weaver, take the weaver farthest to the right.

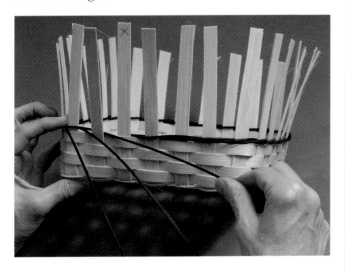

**10.** Moving to the right, as before, weave it in front of two spokes, behind one spoke, and out the space.

**11.** Now take the center weaver and weave in front of two spokes, behind one, and out.

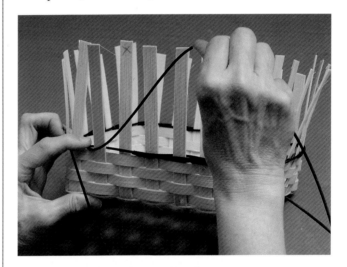

89

**12.** Take the left weaver and bring it in front of two spokes, behind one, and out.

The three weavers are now coming out of the same three spaces from which they began.

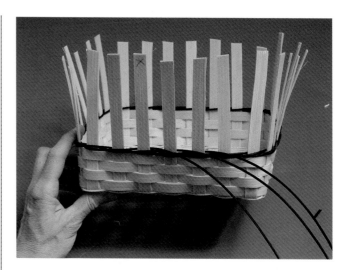

**13.** For the second and final row of weaving, take the weaver farthest to the left and pull it beneath the other two weavers.

**14.** When you pull the left reed beneath the two weavers, you will have woven it in front of two spokes. Now weave it behind one spoke and out.

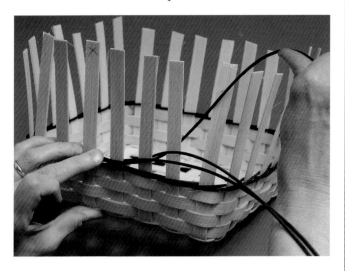

**15.** Continue in the same fashion, always using the weaver farthest to the left.

**16.** Pull the left weaver under the other two weavers and in front of two spokes.

**17.** Finish by weaving it behind a spoke and pulling it out the next space.

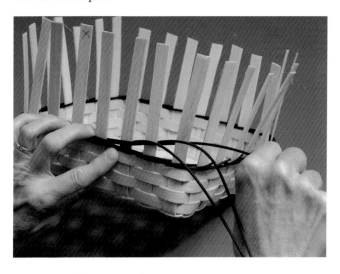

**18.** After a few weaves, the triple arrow pattern becomes visible.

**19.** Continue weaving around the basket until the weavers are coming out the last three spaces before the spoke marked with an X.

**20.** Cut the weavers shorter so they extend about 8 to 10 inches beyond the last spokes.

**21.** Holding the other weavers in place with your thumb, take the weaver on the right and weave it in front of two spokes and under the two weavers already woven in place. Use your packing tool to create a space for the weaver.

**22.** Pull the weaver tight to the inside.

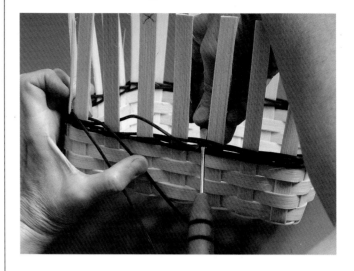

**23.** Repeat with the middle weaver, placing it in front of two spokes and inserting it under two weavers already woven in place.

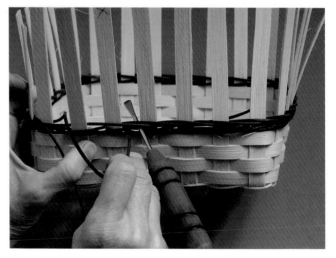

**24.** The final weaver also goes in front of two spokes and beneath two weavers.

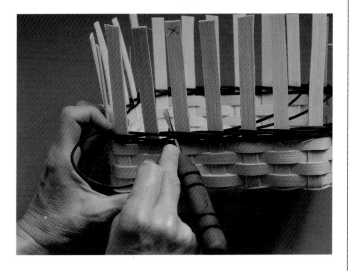

Your basket should now look like this.

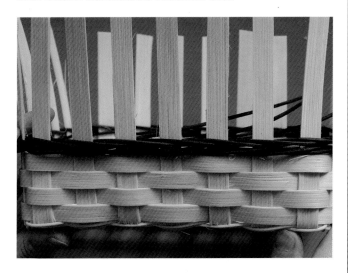

**25.** Trim all of the weavers on the inside of the basket.

**26.** Trim them on the diagonal to about ½ inch so they are behind a spoke.

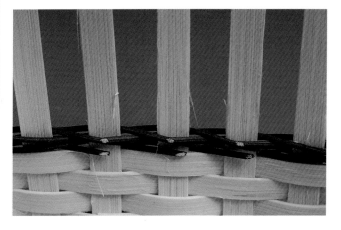

**27.** Now begin another row of weaving with ⅜" flat reed. Start on a spoke at least four spokes from the right corner of the basket. Make sure the first row alternates with the last row of weaving before the triple arrow weave.

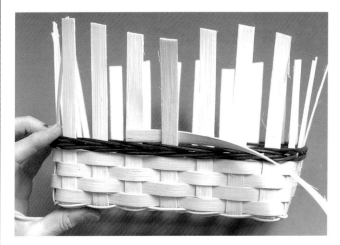

**28.** Add a total of three rows of ⅜" flat weavers, remembering to turn the basket to the next side before beginning a new weaver. Keep the spokes straight and evenly spaced.

The third row of weaving brings the basket to its full height.

**29.** When you've added three rows, pack the rows of weaving and square up your basket.

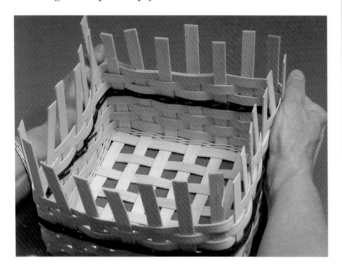

**30.** Wet the tops of the spokes to make them pliable.

**31.** On this basket, every other spoke will be tucked under one weaver. Choose a spoke that ends on the outside of the top row of weaving. Fold the spoke down and trim it off so it will be hidden on the inside of the basket behind the weaver just above the triple arrow weave.

**32.** Push the spoke behind the weaver.

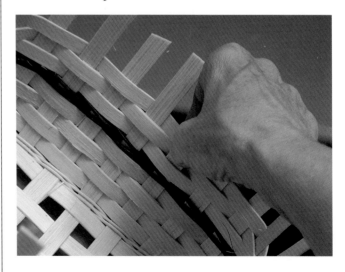

The end of the spoke is hidden behind the weaver.

**33.** Continue to fold over every other spoke, trim it, and tuck it behind the weavers.

**34.** Square your basket.

**35.** Cut off the remaining spokes flush with the top of the basket.

Your basket should now look like this. Next, you will add a rim.

**1.** The rim on this basket will be made the same way as the rim on the bun basket. Wind a piece of ¼" flat reed around the top of your basket three times and cut it. It will be used as the lasher for your rim. Also, wind a piece of ½" flat reed around the top of your basket twice and cut it off about a foot longer. Soak both reeds for several minutes or until flexible before beginning to finish the top of the basket.

**2.** Measure a length of seagrass once around the basket and cut it off a few inches longer. Do not soak the sea-grass.

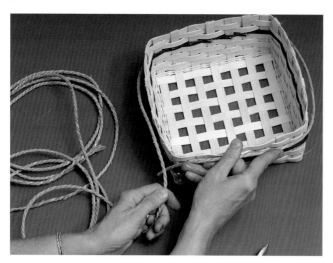

**3.** Pin the ½" rim material to the outside of the top row of weaving, keeping the rough side of the reed against the basket.

**4.** Pin the rim material all the way around the basket.

**5.** Overlap the starting point . . .

**6.** . . . pin it in place and cut the reed so that it overlaps the starting point by four spokes.

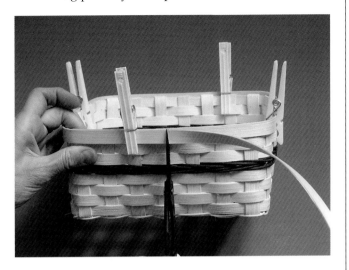

**7.** Begin pinning the seagrass and the inside rim material in place where the outside rim overlap stopped.

**8.** Square at the corners and pin in place.

**9.** Overlap the inside rim and cut it off before the corner.

**10.** Start your lashing just to the right of the inside rim overlap with a fishhook to lock the lashing in place. Refer to the bun basket for instructions on placing the fishhook and lashing the rim.

**11.** Once the fishhook is in place, bring the lasher from the inside over the top of the rim.

97

**12.** Use your packing tool to help insert the lasher underneath the rim in the spoke space to the right of the fishhook. Make sure the smooth side of the lashing is facing the outside. Pull the lasher tight.

**13.** Continue lashing around the basket, using the packing tool as needed.

**14.** Trim the rim ends on the diagonal near a lash, leaving about ⅛ to ¼ inch of rim beyond the lash.

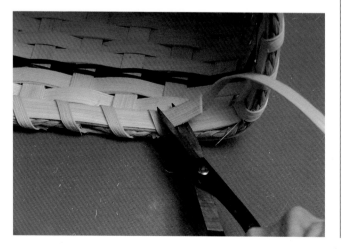

**15.** When your final lashing is in place, lock it in place with another fishhook. It will be in the same place as the first fishhook.

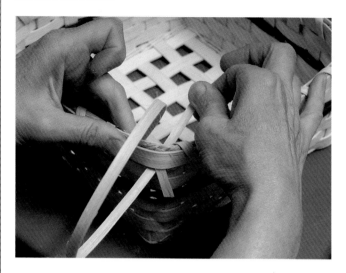

**16.** Insert the end of the lasher from the inside of the basket between the seagrass and the outer rim. Pull tight.

**17.** Now insert the lasher between the seagrass and the outer rim and the outside of the top row of weaving. Pull tight.

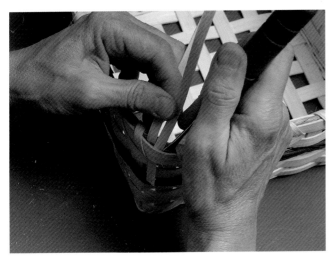

**18.** Trim each fishhook flush with the base of the rim.

**19.** Your basket will look like this when the rim is in place. You could consider your basket complete at this step or you could fill in the base of your basket using the following technique.

**1.** Soak one length of ¼" flat reed for several minutes until flexible. Slide the end of the reed underneath the entire width of an overlapping spoke next to a corner at the bottom of the basket.

**2.** Cut the reed so that it will slide underneath the spoke at the edge of the bottom, as shown.

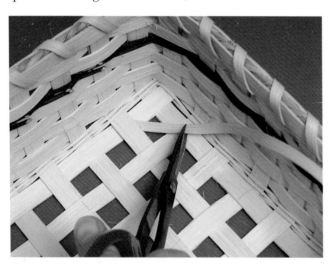

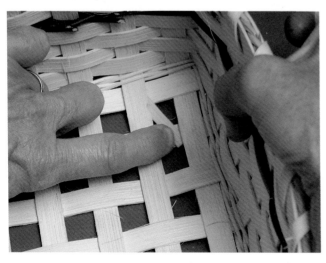

The first small piece of reed is in place.

**3.** Continue cutting and placing flat reed strips diagonally across the basket bottom.

**4.** On the second row, tuck the weaver between the center spoke intersections first and under the end spokes last.

**5.** Continue weaving between the center spoke intersections and tucking the weaver tails under the spokes on the sides of the basket.

**6.** Work from one corner of the basket to the other.

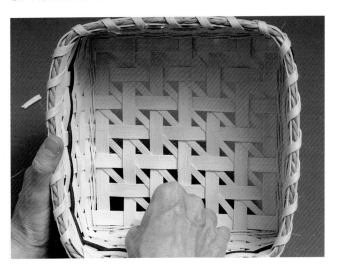

The bottom of the basket looks like this when complete.

101

# 4

# Easter Basket

For our final project, we'll make a beautiful Easter basket. With this project, you will learn how to weave a round base with round reed, and you will learn a new style for finishing a basket rim.

**GETTING STARTED**
Materials needed to complete this project include:

> ⅜" flat reed for the spokes and rim
> 6" D handle
> #2 round reed to weave the bottom of the basket
> ¼" flat reed to weave the side of the basket
> One piece each of ¼" flat reed in orange, blue, and yellow for the side
> One piece of ½" flat reed in purple for the side

## Twining a Round Base

**1.** From the ⅜" flat reed, cut nine spokes 22 inches long and two handle spokes 8 inches long Soak the 22-inch spokes for five to ten minutes until pliable.

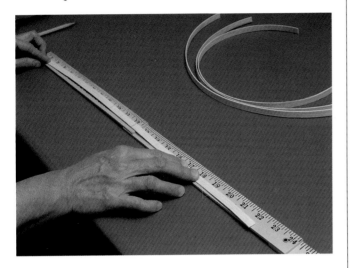

**2.** Mark four of the 22-inch spokes at the center of the rough side with a pencil. Also mark them at 1¼ inches on each side of the center mark. The center mark will be at 11 inches and the other marks will be at 9¾ inches and 12¼ inches. These marks will guide the first row of weaving. Keep the rough side of the spokes—and the pencil marks—facing the inside of the basket.

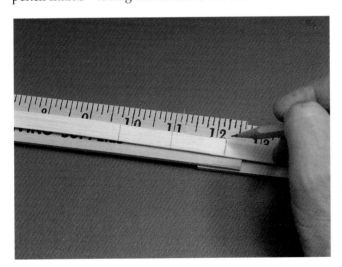

**3.** Mark the handle at the center and 1¼ inches to each side of the center mark: at 3 inches, 1¾ inches, and 4¼ inches.

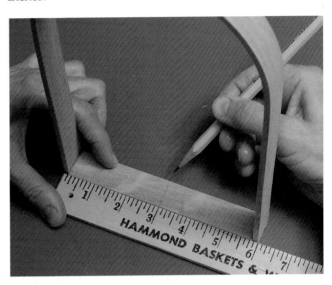

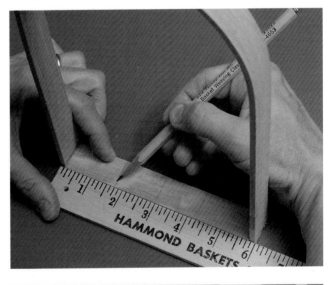

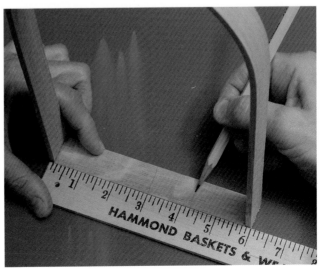

**4.** After soaking a long piece of #2 round reed for five to ten minutes, loop it so that it is about 6 inches longer than the other.

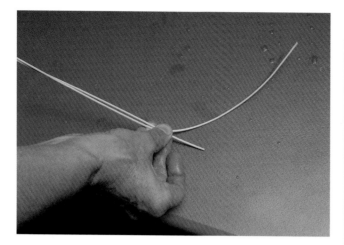

**5.** Use a crimping tool to crimp the round reed near the center of the loop, keeping one end about 6 inches longer. Crimping it makes the reed less likely to break when it is folded.

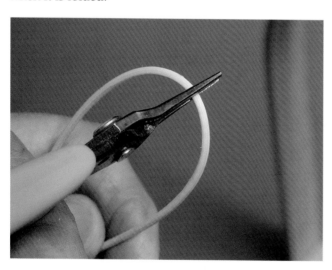

The crimped reed will look like this.

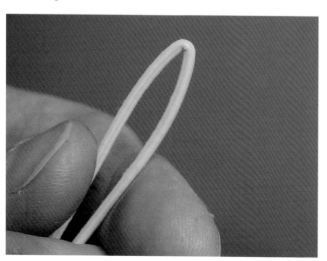

**6.** Place two of the marked spokes in an X pattern across the handle, keeping the center marks to the center of the handle.

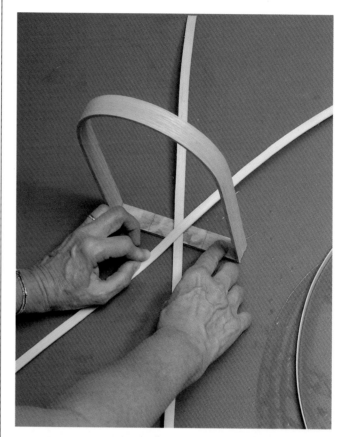

**7.** Add the third and fourth spokes, again lining up the center marks at the center of the handle.

Space the spokes evenly like the spokes in a wheel.

**8.** Mark the end of one spoke with an X and loop the piece of #2 reed around it. (Any of the spokes can be used.)

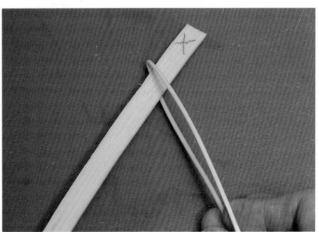

**9.** Holding all the spokes together with one hand, with the other hand pull the round reed to the 1¼-inch pencil mark on the spoke to begin twining around the base on the pencil marks.

**10.** Start with the weaver on the bottom. Lay it on the mark on the top of the next spoke.

**11.** Pick up the other weaver. Weave it under the second spoke. Hold it in place with your finger.

**12.** Weave it on top of the next spoke at the pencil mark.

**13.** Continue to alternate the weavers, twining under and over with each and making sure the reed not being woven stays to the inside. Hold the weaving in place with your fingers as you work.

**14.** Pull the reed that weaves on top of the handle all the way through the handle.

**15.** Weave the other reed under the handle and on top of the next spoke. Go back to the reed that wove on top of the handle and weave it under the next spoke and on top of the following spoke. Always keep the reed not being woven to the inside.

**16.** Continue twining around the base, keeping the initial row of twining on the pencil marks.

**17.** When you begin the second row of twining, make sure your twining alternates like this. If it doesn't, undo the weave back to the mistake and fix it.

**18.** Continue the second row weaving under and over with each weaver and then switching.

**19.** Keep weaving to fill in the bottom of the basket. When your reed is down to a few inches, it's time to tuck it in and begin a new reed.

**20.** Crimp the reed at a place where it is coming up from under a spoke and just before it goes over the next spoke.

**21.** Cut the reed on the diagonal, leaving about ⅜ inch of reed beyond the crimp.

**22.** Tuck the reed in along the edge of the spoke using your packing tool and your finger.

**23.** Crimp the end of a new #2 round reed and cut it on the diagonal to about ⅜ inch beyond the crimp.

**24.** Insert the end of the reed beside the spoke that is immediately before the spoke where you tucked the last reed.

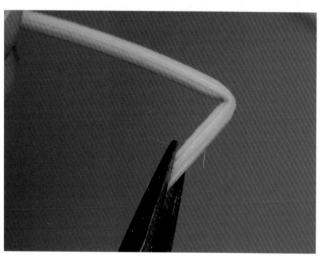

110

**25.** This method hides the start and finish of the reed. By looking closely, both ends can be seen here to the right of the center spoke.

**26.** Once you weave a few more spokes, your second reed will be at an end. Finish it in the same way and begin another new weaver.

**27.** Tuck in the end of the reed before beginning a new reed.

**28.** Continue weaving six rows of twining. Your basket should look like this. Make sure you end on the spoke marked with the X. Now it's time to add the remaining five spokes.

## Adding Spokes

**1.** Start by laying a new spoke across the center of the spokes and underneath both round reed weavers, as shown.

**2.** Push the spoke until it lines up with the ends of the other spokes. Center it between the two spokes to which you're adding it. Make sure the rough side of the spoke faces up toward the inside of the basket.

**3.** Once you've added the new spoke, twine it twice, once in front of the spoke and once after the spoke.

112

**4.** Add another spoke in the next space, pushing it under the weavers. Line it up with the ends of the other spokes and center it between the spokes to either side.

**5.** Twine the new spoke in place by taking the back weaver under one spoke and on top of the next, then taking the back weaver again and weaving it under one spoke and on top of the next.

**6.** Continue to add spokes until all are in place.

**7.** As you weave around the base of the basket, you will anchor both ends of the spokes in place.

**8.** After one revolution, make sure the spaces between the spokes are even.

**9.** Keep weaving around the base.

The base is off-center from the handle and one side has filled in with twining while the other side has not.

**WRONG**

**10.** Tap the basket handle with the side of your fist to slide the base into place.

The twining is centered on the basket handle.

**RIGHT**

**11.** Keep twining until the handle is filled in and you have a 6-inch base to your basket.

**12.** The last row of twining may stack on the inside of the handle.

**13.** When you get back to the starting spoke with the X, measure to make sure the base is 6 inches wide.

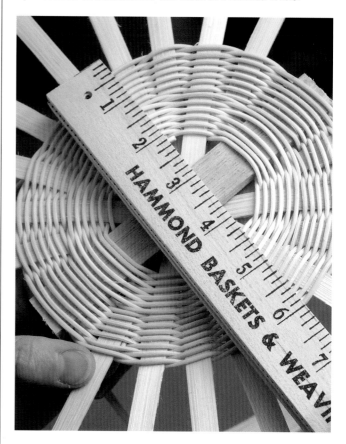

**14.** Trim off the weavers on a short diagonal so they end on top of a spoke.

The basket bottom is complete.

**15.** Wet the spokes at the base of the basket.

**16.** When the spokes are flexible, crease each spoke tight to the twining.

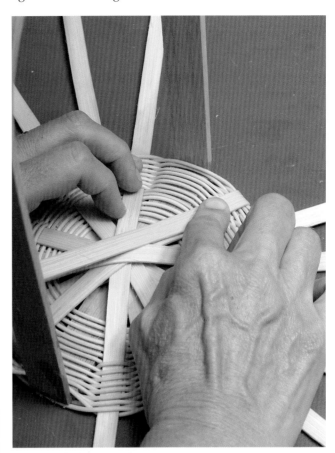

117

# Weaving a Pattern with Dyed Reed

**1.** Soak the ¼" natural flat reed for five to ten minutes until flexible. Beginning at the middle of one side, start weaving with it at the base of the basket. Make sure that the smooth side of the reed is always facing outside. Begin so that the first weaver is on the outside of the handle.

**2.** Pin the first row of weaving in place to keep it tight to the twining on the base.

**3.** Weave over one spoke and under the next.

**4.** Overlap the first weaver by four spokes and cut it off so the end will be hidden by a spoke.

**5.** Shift one-quarter of the way around the basket to begin your next weaver. Counting the handle as a spoke, start two spokes past where the first weaver ended. This ensures that all the weavers don't begin and end in the same place and results in a more balanced basket.

**6.** Continually adjust the spokes to be straight and evenly spaced.

119

**7.** After you complete two rows of weaving using the natural reed, pack it tight starting with the bottom row.

**8.** Measure a piece of ¼" flat orange reed by wrapping it around the basket, leaving at least enough extra to overlap by four spokes. Soak the orange reed for a minute or two and dry it with a towel so the color doesn't bleed.

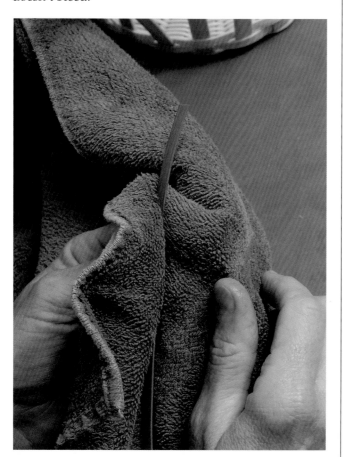

**9.** Begin the orange reed two spokes from where the last natural reed ended.

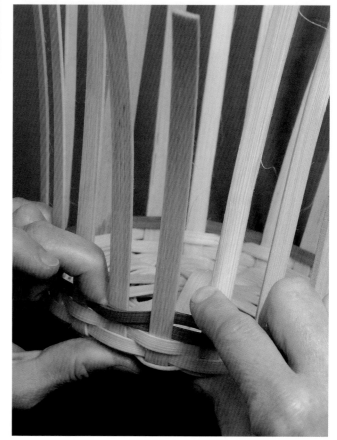

**10.** Weave it over and under around the basket and overlap by four spokes.

**11.** Use the same technique with a blue reed, again starting two spokes from where the orange reed ended.

**12.** Next weave in a yellow reed.

**13.** Add the ½" flat purple reed using the same technique. Notice how the sides of the basket are straight and not flared. If the sides should begin to flare, you may need to unweave one or more reeds and weave them back in place, making sure that the spokes are straight up.

**14.** Repeat the color pattern in reverse, adding a yellow reed followed by a blue reed and an orange reed.

Your basket should now look like this.

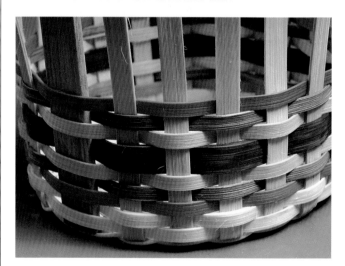

**15.** Once the dyed reeds are in place, add two more rows of natural ¼" flat reed, again starting each row two spokes past the end of the previous row of weaving.

**16.** After the last row has been woven, pack weavers tightly with the packing tool, starting with the bottom row and working your way up the basket.

## Finishing the Basket Rim

**1.** Measure the piece of ⅜" rim to go around the basket one and one-quarter times. Soak the rim material and the two 8-inch flared spokes for five to ten minutes.

**2.** Wet the ends of the basket spokes so they are pliable and can be folded.

**3.** Dry off the dyed reeds if they become wet when soaking the spokes.

**4.** Add an 8-inch spoke on the outside of the handle on both sides, placing it behind the weavers.

**5.** Use your packing tool to help place the spoke. These spokes will be used to secure the rim in place.

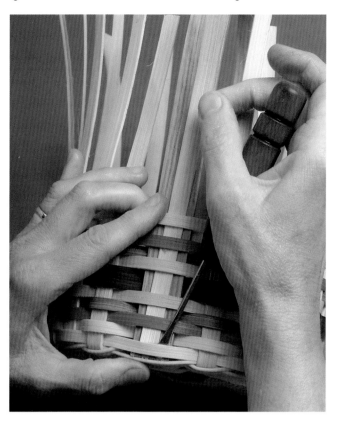

**6.** Take the rim piece and pin it around the basket inside the spokes. Begin on the middle of one side and place the rim about ¼ inch above the weaving.

**7.** At the handle, place the rim material between the outside of the handle and the extra spoke.

**8.** Cut off the rim material so it overlaps about four spokes.

**9.** Starting with the spoke just to the right of the rim overlap, fold it down gently and bring it out the space between it and the next spoke.

**10.** Pull the spoke down until it is fairly tight.

**11.** Now fold it up so it crosses the next spoke.

**12.** Take it to the second spoke and cut it off so it will be hidden behind the spoke.

Leave the end fairly long so that more than half of the spoke covers it.

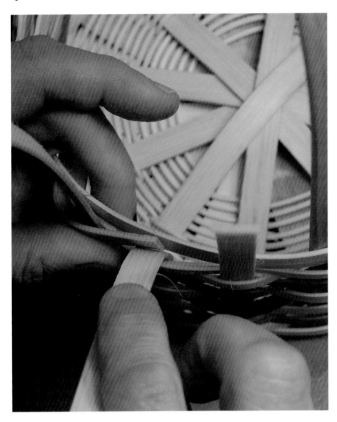

**13.** Take the next spoke, fold it down gently, and weave it in the same way. Weave it beneath the spoke you just folded to the outside of the basket.

**14.** Pull the spoke fairly tight. Fold it across the spokes to the right and cut it to hide behind the second spoke.

**15.** Continue folding and tucking spokes around the basket.

**16.** Cut the spoke to be hidden behind the handle spoke just a little longer, because the handle spoke has a tendency to pull to the right.

**17.** When you get back to the rim overlap, make sure that the tail of the rim is behind the spoke.

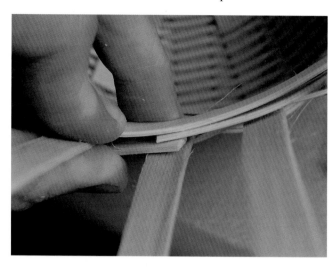

**18.** When the overlap has been secured with the spoke, cut the end of the rim material diagonally close to the folded spoke.

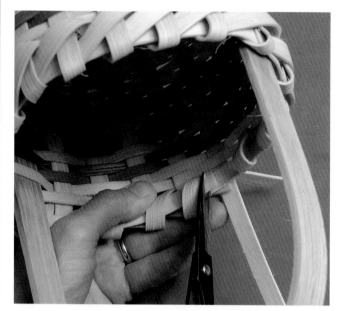

**19.** The last two spokes need to be worked behind already folded spokes.

**20.** Use your packing tool if necessary to squeeze the spoke ends into place.

Your finished basket should look like this.

# 5

# How to Dye Reed

Each of the projects in this book use dyed reed as accents.

Dyed reed can be purchased in many colors. But it is fairly easy to dye your own. Not only can you choose the colors you want, you can mix and match the types and quantities of reed you dye.

## GETTING STARTED

Tools and materials needed to dye reed include:

> a kettle that can hold several
>> gallons of water
> a package of fabric dye
> vinegar
> reed to be dyed
> a long-handled wooden spoon
> rubber gloves
> a long stick or pole on which to
>> drape the dyed reed while it
>> dries
> a plastic tub that holds several
>> gallons of water

*Fabric dye is available in many colors.*

130

While reed can be dyed indoors, it works best as an outdoor project. This old propane grill has been adapted to use for dyeing reed.

**1.** Pour about two gallons of water, or enough to completely cover the reed, into your kettle. Bring the water to a boil.

**2.** Once the water comes to a boil, carefully pour in the package of dye.

**3.** Stir it well with a wooden spoon to completely dissolve the dye. Turn the heat to low.

**4.** If using a whole package of reed, cut open all ties except the end tie, which will hold the reed in place while it is dyed.

**5.** Add the reed to the boiling water.

**6.** Submerge the reed completely in the dye bath.

132

**7.** Let the reed soak for ten to fifteen minutes.

**8.** Put on your rubber gloves. Use the wooden spoon to help flip the reed to the other side. Leave it in the dye bath another ten to fifteen minutes or until it is the desired shade, keeping in mind that the dried color will be lighter.

**9.** Once the reed is the desired color, use the wooden spoon to remove the reed from the water.

**10.** Hang it to dry on the stick. This stick has been placed on two saw horses.

**11.** Spread out the reed so it can dry easily. Don't let it touch the ground.

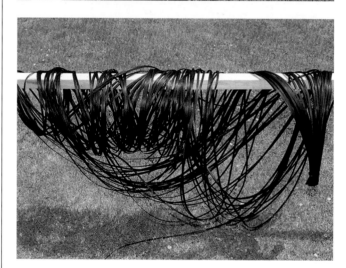

134

**1.** After the dyed reed has dried completely, which can take several hours to a day or two, put about two gallons of cold water into a large plastic tub.

**2.** Add about ½ cup of vinegar to the water to set the color.

**3.** Submerge the dyed reed into the water.

**4.** Once the reed has soaked in the vinegar water for at least forty-five minutes, take it out.

**5.** Spread the reed on the pole to dry. Once it has dried completely, it can be rolled back up and stored until needed.

# Resources

## BASKET MAKING SUPPLIES

Allen's Basketworks, Inc.
760-320-4467
*www.allensbasketworks.com*

Arnie's Arts n Crafts
3741 W Houghton Lake Drive
Houghton Lake, MI 48629
800-563-2356
*www.basketpatterns.com*

Baskets of Joy
21 Old Bath Road
Brunswick, ME 04011
800-377-6097
*www.basketsofjoy.com*

BasketWeavingSupplies.com
866-928-5430
*www.basketweavingsupplies.com*

The Country Seat, Inc.
1013 Old Philly Pike
Kempton, PA 19529
610-756-6124
*www.countryseat.com*

H.H. Perkins Co.
222 Universal Drive
North Haven, CT 06473
800-462-6660
*www.hhperkins.com*

North Carolina Basket Works
130 Main Street
Vass, NC 28394
800-338-4972
*www.ncbasketworks.com*

Royalwood, Ltd.
517 Woodville Road
Mansfield, OH 44907
800-526-1630
*www.royalwoodltd.com*

V. I. Reed & Cane, Inc.
800-852-0025
*www.basketweaving.com*

For just about any information dealing with baskets, check out the website *www.basketmakers.com*.

For more how-to information on basket weaving, visit *www.basket-making.com*.